Tsawalk

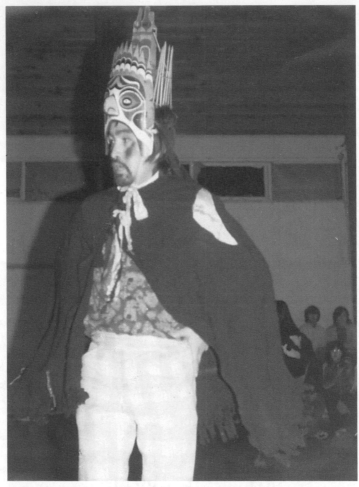

Author in regalia, doing the Clax-sawta dance in Thunderbird Hall, Ahousaht, mid-1970s.

Tsawalk

A Nuu-chah-nulth Worldview

Umeek ❋ *E. Richard Atleo*

UBCPress · Vancouver · Toronto

22 21 20 19 18   11

Printed in Canada on acid-free paper.

National Library of Canada Cataloguing in Publication

Atleo, Eugene Richard, 1939-
    Tsawalk : a Nuu-chah-nulth worldview / E. Richard Atleo (Umeek).

    Includes bibliographical references and index.
    ISBN 0-7748-1084-X (bound); ISBN 0-7748-1085-8 (pbk.)

    1. Nootka Indians – Religion. 2. Nootka philosophy. 3. Creation – Mythology – British Columbia – Vancouver Island. 4. Indian philosophy – British Columbia – Vancouver Island. I. Title.

E99.N85A84 2004   299.7'8955   C2004-900687-8

Canadä

UBC Press gratefully acknowledges the financial support for our publishing program of the Government of Canada through the Book Publishing Industry Development Program (BPIDP), and of the Canada Council for the Arts, and the British Columbia Arts Council.

This book has been published with the help of a grant from the Canadian Federation for the Humanities and Social Sciences, through the Aid to Scholarly Publications Programme, using funds provided by the Social Sciences and Humanities Research Council of Canada, and with the help of the K.D. Srivastava Fund.

Printed and bound in Canada by Friesens
Set in Stone by Artegraphica Design Co. Ltd.
Copy editor: Robert Lewis
Proofreader: Jillian Shoichet
Indexer: Christine Jacobs
Cartographer: Eric Leinberger

UBC Press
The University of British Columbia
2029 West Mall
Vancouver, BC V6T 1Z2
604-822-5959 / Fax: 604-822-6083
www.ubcpress.ca

This book is dedicated to my ancestors,

*who knew how to **tloo-qua-nah**.*

May their legacy thrive.

Contents

Acknowledgments

I wish to acknowledge the encouragement and knowledgeable help of family members: my mother, Elsie Robinson (formerly Atleo, née Little); my late grandmother Margaret Atleo and her spouse, Teddy George, also deceased; my late uncle Mark Atleo; my aunt Trudy and her husband, Edwin, also known as Qwascha-a; my aunts Flossie and Nora; and my wife Marlene, ?eh ?eh naa tuu kwiss.

I also wish to acknowledge the assistance of Jean Wilson and Darcy Cullen of UBC Press as well as of anonymous reviewers, without which the publication of this manuscript would not have been possible.

Prologue
My Great-Grandfather Keesta

Every protocol had been observed between the whaling chief and the spirit of the whale. Keesta had thrown the harpoon, and the whale had accepted it, had grabbed and held onto the harpoon according to the agreement they had made through prayers and petitions. Harmony prevailed, whaler and whale were one, *heshook-ish tsawalk*.

All of a sudden something went wrong, some disharmony arose, some disunity intruded, and the whale turned and began to tow Keesta and his paddlers straight off shore. Keesta took inventory. Everyone in the whaling canoe remained true to the protocols – cleansed, purified, and in harmony. Prayer songs intensified. Still, the great whale refused to turn toward the beach, heading straight off shore. Keesta and the paddlers had kept true to their agreements, and now there seemed nothing left to do except to cut the *atlu*, the rope attached to the whale.

Keesta took his knife, and as he moved to cut the rope, Ah-up-wha-eek (Wren) landed on the whale and spoke to Keesta: "Tell the whale to go back to where it was harpooned." Keesta spoke to the whale, and immediately the great whale turned according to the word of Wren, the little brown bird, and returned to where it was first harpooned, and there it died.

After the whale had been towed ashore, Keesta discovered, as he had suspected, that the disharmony and disunity had intruded at home. When his wife had heard that the whale had taken the harpoon, she had roused herself and prematurely broken away from her ritual in order to make welcome preparations. At the point when she began to go about her life in disharmony from the rest was exactly when the great whale had begun to tow Keesta and his paddlers off shore.

Introduction

Development of an Indigenous Theory

In the Nuu-chah-nulth language, *heshook-ish tsawalk* means "everything is one." *Heshook-ish tsawalk* is a Nuu-chah-nulth perspective that is inclusive of all reality, both physical and metaphysical.[1] It is the thesis of this book and consequently the basis for the development of an indigenous theory. *Heshook-ish tsawalk* poses the theoretical proposition that everything is one. Thus it is called the theory of Tsawalk. The notion that all things are one stems directly from assumptions found in Nuu-chah-nulth origin stories that predate the conscious historical notion of civilization and scientific progress. This theory provides another interpretation about the nature of existence based on Nuu-chah-nulth origin stories in contrast to the nature of existence suggested by origin stories that are evolution-based.

Clement C.J. Webb in *A History of Philosophy* maintains that modern civilization begins with "leaving off telling tales" (Webb 1959, 9). That is, according to this philosopher, modern civilization could not begin until people turned away from their ancient origin "tales" and began to think in scientific terms. In contrast to this view, the theory of Tsawalk not only begins with these "tales," or origin stories, but also depends on these "tales" both as the foundation of knowledge about the state of existence and as a guide for its interpretation. *Heshook-ish tsawalk* (everything is one) is a common idea today, particularly in the environmental movement, and for this reason I try to explain and clarify some of its traditional meanings.[2] *Heshook-ish tsawalk* means more than the unity of the physical universe. It means more than the empirically based meaning attached to the word "holism."

"We are holistic thinkers too!" a professor at the University of British Columbia declared somewhat defensively. No doubt holistic thinking that assumes the unity of the spiritual and physical domains of reality has always played some part in Western thought. Yet, from an outsider's perspective such as mine, I find it doubtful that holistic thinking could be considered an overriding theme in patterns of Western thought. There is instead a prevailing tendency to compartmentalize experience and thus assume that some parts have no relationship to other parts. For example, in *Philosophers on Education: Six Essays on the Foundations of Western Thought,* the authors state: "The world abounds in separations which have been overdone, which ignore the basic character of the experiential continuum. Thus are separated school and society, child and curriculum, method and subject matter, to name a few with immediate educational significance. The separations are useful, even vital, but imply no final disconnection" (Brumbaugh and Lawrence 1963, 136).

The "experiential continuum" in education is fragmented first between school and society and then into myriad departments and knowledge disciplines, just as it is fragmented into myriad categories within the social, political, and economic dimensions of human existence. These separations are useful, declare the authors, but the "experiential continuum" seems to have been forgotten or ignored.

John Ralston Saul provides another perspective on the fragmentation phenomena observed in Western philosophy. He argues that in spite of the different labels attached to various "ages" (Reason, Enlightenment, and Romanticism) in the Western world, the past 500 years may be called the Age of Reason. The "Dictatorship of Reason," he argues, has virtually excluded other equally important human characteristics: "Reason began, abruptly, to separate itself from and to outdistance the other more or less recognized human characteristics – spirit, appetite, faith and emotion, but also intuition, will and, most important, experience. This gradual encroachment on the foreground continues today. It has reached a degree of imbalance so extreme that the mythological importance of reason obscures all else and has driven the other elements into the marginal frontiers of doubtful respectability" (Saul 1993, 15).

Reason, or rationality, is a cornerstone of science. Saul does not argue against reason but against what he considers to be an "extreme" emphasis on it, almost to the exclusion of other human characteristics that may be termed metaphysical, such as spirit and faith. The implication, from my perspective, is that reason, or human cognition, may not be the sole source of knowledge, that "faith and spirit" may also play a significant and alternative role to human reason.

What is the source of this imbalance between reason and spirit? The imbalance can be traced to scientific methodology. In *Wisdom of the Elders,* Peter Knudtson and David Suzuki state:

Werner Heisenberg discovered that we could never know what Nature is like because in order to observe it, we have to pin it down and thus change it; Niels Bohr found that the properties of subatomic particles could be described only by probability, never with absolute certainty. Parts of nature and other systems were shown to interact *synergistically* so that the behavior and properties of a system as a whole cannot be predicted on the basis of what is known about its individual components. Thus, while science yields powerful insights into isolated fragments of the world, the sum total of these insights is a disconnected, inadequate description of the whole. (Knudtson and Suzuki 1992, xxii)

Werner Heisenberg identifies two limitations of science in the above quotation: first, "Nature" it seems does not hold still for the research scientist so that reliable data reflective of nature can be collected; second, the methodology of science is predicated upon reductionism and the examination of isolated variables, which "yields powerful insights into isolated fragments of the world," but the sum of which is only a fragmented description of reality. The need to focus on isolated variables automatically obscures any assumption about the general nature of inter-relationships and connections between variables, obscures what Robert Brumbraugh and Nathaniel Lawrence call the "experiential continuum." In addition, scientific experimentation that finds no significant relationship between variables directly implies fragmentation, although it does not necessarily prove that this is the case. Nevertheless, if two variables are found not to be related, does this use of language not indicate that the universe is fragmented according to scientific criteria? Not only does this use of language, "not significantly related," reflect a scientific view of existence, but it is also reflected generally in the fragmentation of Western thought – in the separation of church and state, for example – and furthermore in Western policies and practices.

Some scientists have recognized this uncertainty about whether or not the universe can be in a state of fragmentation. Recent discoveries in physics now challenge earlier ideas that space and physical objects are separate. It turns out that they are not. Einstein's theory of relativity says that matter cannot be separated from its field of gravity (Capra 1991, 231). This theory shattered the nineteenth-century assumption that space and matter are separate. Fritjof Capra maintains that the reality of the universe is not so much described by matter and space as by a quantum field in which are found local condensations of particles (matter), or concentrations of energy that come and go, "dissolving into the underlying [quantum] field" (ibid.). The universe can more accurately be described as a quantum field that is present everywhere in space and yet in its particle aspect has a discontinuous, granular structure. The universe is, therefore, not space and matter according to the old scientific paradigm but a quantum field. Capra concludes: "Thus modern physics shows us ... that material objects are not distinct entities, but are inseparably linked to their environment; that their properties can only be understood in terms of their interaction with the rest of the world" (ibid., 231).

From my perspective it appears that science, in order to gain some insight into the world, began first by isolating fragments of it and studying these in relation to other isolated fragments (known as variables) but then discovered through physics that knowledge of isolated fragments cannot completely explain what Brumbaugh and Lawrence have called the "experiential continuum," or the dynamic nature of existence. Thomas Berry provides another example related to this discussion about recent findings in physics:

> The unity of the entire complex of galactic systems is among the most basic experience of contemporary physics. It is especially important in this discussion to recognize the unity of the total process, from that first unimaginable moment of cosmic emergence through all its subsequent forms of expression until the present. This unbreakable bond of relatedness that makes of the whole a universe becomes increasingly apparent to scientific formulation or understanding. In virtue of this relatedness, everything is intimately present to everything else in the universe. Nothing is completely itself without everything else. (Berry 1988, 91)

The new findings about the nature of the universe describe empirical reality as concentrations of energy that can dissolve into the underlying quantum field, and these same findings indicate that "everything is intimately present to everything else in the universe." In other words, material objects are no longer perceived as independent entities but rather as "local condensations" of the quantum field or as "concentrations of energy" that are totally dependent upon, and inseparable from, the field. Empirical reality is more than meets the scientific eye. Underlying an unbelievably diverse creation of matter and life forms is a quantum field that appears to be a common source of experience. This new scientific paradigm may have far-reaching effects.

The corollary to the old view about an empirically observable universe is the assumption that human cognition or reason alone is required to

Figure 1

Plato's three worlds

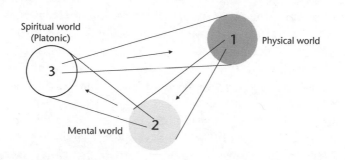

Source: Adapted from Penrose 1993.

advance knowledge and discover truth. Webb's view that civilization could not progress until tribal myths were discarded rejects the metaphysical viewpoint embedded in these myths in favour of scientific reason. There is no question that human reason has an enormous capacity to discover and advance knowledge. In question is its presumed supremacy in, and exclusive rights to, knowledge acquisition.

The assumption that knowledge is acquired only through human reason may be predicated upon the worldview that primary experience is physical or empirical and that other experiences are secondary. An extreme interpretation of this view is that all spiritual reality is simply an imaginary creation of the human mind. All extraordinary human experiences that cannot be explained by empirical means are mere delusions or figments of human imagination. This assumption can now be challenged from the vantage point of the new physics.

Curiously, or ironically, the mathematician Roger Penrose, as an apt metaphor to explain the mysterious relationship between the Platonic mathematical world, the physical world, and the mental world, invokes Plato's forms. Although Penrose does not claim that the physical world arises from the Platonic world, only that it is intimately related, he acknowledges that Plato himself would have insisted that the world of perfect forms (mathematical in this case) is primary.

As Penrose says: "In some way, each of the three worlds, the Platonic mathematical, the physical, and the mental, seems mysteriously to 'emerge' from – or at least to be intimately related to – a small part of its predecessor (the worlds being taken cyclically)" (Penrose 1993, 416).

Plato was certain that a world of perfect forms existed independently of the human mind. What Penrose seeks is mathematical truth. Where do the forms come from? Do they arise purely from the mind or independently from some other source? Penrose ultimately speculates that "our mathematical understanding might result from some unfathomable algorithm" (ibid., 144) and consequently concludes that "whatever brain activity is responsible for consciousness (at least in this particular manifestation) it must depend upon a physics that lies beyond computational simulation" (ibid., 411).

Richard Tarnas, in *The Passion of the Western Mind: Understanding the Ideas That Have Shaped Our World View,* suggests that an unnatural separation between the human mind and heart/soul/spirit has taken place in Western philosophy, a sort of cultural and psychic lobotomy. The preeminence of human cognition, or reason, in Western culture constrains humans to focus on physical experience, subsuming soul, or spirit. If all truth is essentially empirical, then cognition alone is sufficient. However, if experience is more than empirical, human reason by itself may be insufficient to access the whole of existence. To be sure, human reason is necessary for human consciousness, and it is the only scientifically known means of human understanding. Nevertheless, it is possible that the human brain, in addition to being an active cognition centre, may also be an important *information-coordinating centre.*

In the same way that Plato assumed the primacy of perfect forms over the physical world, the theory of Tsawalk discussed in this book assumes a spiritual primacy to existence. Creation, the physical world, is considered a manifestation or reflection (as in a shadow or image) of its spiritual Creator. The physical universe is like an insubstantial shadow of the actual, substantial Creator. In this worldview, the highest form of cognition, of consciousness, does not occur in the insubstantial, shadowlike physical realm, but in the realm of creation's spiritual source.

It is the same type of issue faced by Copernicus in the sixteenth century. The earth is no more the centre of the solar system than human cognition or reason is necessarily the centre of knowledge and truth. Just as Copernicus discovered that the earth is not the centre of the universe, so too might human reason be found not to be the primary source of knowledge and truth. This notion is part of the theory of Tsawalk. Human understanding may be part of a larger and greater understanding, the sum of which makes up Qua-ootz, the Nuu-chah-nulth Creator, Owner of Reality. Black Elk, an Oglala Sioux holy man, indicates this in the following account of Crazy Horse's vision:

Crazy Horse's father was my father's cousin, and there were no chiefs in our family before Crazy Horse; but there were holy men; and he became a chief because of the power he got in a vision when he was a boy. When I was a man, my father told me something about that vision. Of course he did not know all of it; but he said that Crazy Horse dreamed and went into the world where there is nothing but the spirits of all things. That is the real world that is behind this one, and everything we see here is something like a shadow from that world. (Neihardt 1972, 85)

If the empirical reality we perceive is more like a "shadow" of the actual reality of the spiritual dimension, then one assumption of "hard" science is thrown into question. Is there more to existence than that discovered by empirical science? Is it possible that scientific discoveries are not of the first order of existence but of a second order? In Janet Hodgson and Jay Kothare's *Vision Quest: Native Spirituality and the Church in Canada*, Andrew Ahenakew, a contemporary Anglican priest of Cree descent, relates his vision as follows:

"I went to bed, I don't know what time, but I think it must have been about 1 o'clock, 2 o'clock, somewhere around that time. I saw something coming from the river way, from the north. When I looked again I was sitting on the bed. I knew I was sitting on the bed but I guess I was sleeping. That motel seemed to have no walls. This creature came right towards me. He stopped about six feet from me, maybe a little closer, and he looked at me and smiled. A beautiful creature, a creature of God. And he spoke to me. The creature said, 'I have been sent here by the higher power. I'm sent to come and instruct you to make medicine, which will be yours. If I tell you what to do and you listen.' I thought to myself, how can I listen, when I'm a clergyman, to this creature?"

The bear could read his thoughts and told him that even though he did not believe now, he would believe later and would do this big thing. The bear smiled, showing teeth four to five inches long, and continued: "I'm sent here to come and teach you how to make medicine. I'm willing to give my body to be killed so that you can take me and use me for medicine." (Hodgson and Kothare 1990, 120-21)

Andrew Ahenakew was unaware of his physical state. He didn't know whether he was awake or asleep. The subordination of the physical realm to the spiritual realm is indicated by the fact that in this experience the motel appears to have no walls. The walls, so to speak, have dissolved into the underlying quantum field. Moreover, the bear was not even standing on the floor but stood suspended in mid-air. Human thoughts that are invisible to other humans were visible to this spiritual being. The mission of the bear was to provide information about medicine for human illness. Although Ahenakew, at first, refused to obey the bear for fear of ridicule and expulsion by his superiors, he eventually spent many successful years healing specific illnesses identified by the bear. These kinds of spiritual experiences that manifest empirical results can have implications for the primacy of the spiritual realm over the physical. Moreover, the bear explicitly told Andrew that "when this world was created, all creation was perfect at the beginning of time" (ibid., 129).

Such is also the position of this book. I will consider the place of science and the nature of creation in the light of indigenous origin stories. For example, as a cognition centre the brain is associated with memory activity. However, sources of power external to the human being may also contribute to the process of memory. Black Elk provides one account of this phenomenon in John G. Neihardt's *Black Elk Speaks:*

> It was the pictures I remembered and the words that went with them; for nothing I have ever seen with my eyes was so clear and bright as what my vision showed me; and no words that I have ever heard with my ears were like the words I heard. *I did not have to remember these things; they have remembered themselves all these years.* It was as I grew older that the meanings came clearer and clearer out of the pictures and the words; and even now I know that more was shown to me than I can tell. (Neihardt 1972, 49, emphasis added)

It is usual in human memory experience for events long past to fade, but in this case an old man is speaking of a vision that took place when he was nine. Not only is his memory intact, but the vision's meaning becomes clearer with time. Specific memory recall is not necessarily unusual as people approach the end of life, but what is unusual is the orientation of the memory recall. Black Elk testifies that his recollection of his vision did not depend upon his own cognitive ability but rather had an independent power of its own. The spiritual source of memory of the vision, quite apart from Black Elk's memory, ensured Black Elk's recollection of it. This type of recollection is unusual (Zechmeister and Nyberg 1981; Eysenck 1984; Parkin 1987). A memory that comes from outside human memory banks must remain theoretical. Nevertheless, this example about the extent of memory beyond the empirical domain extends the dialogue about the nature of existence.

Today there is some question about the surety of the foundation upon which Western civilization is built. John Ralston Saul observes that "since the mid-sixties, however, there has been a growing general sense that our systems are not working. Multiple signs of this are easily identified, but they somehow resist fitting into a pattern. The depression. The swollen armaments industry. The breakdown of the legal system ... Random examples from an endless list" (Saul 1993, 21).

Peace, order, and good government as ideals of Western civilization have not been practically realized. In fact, there are local, regional, and global conflicts and environmental devastation to the entire planet, and good government is the exception rather than the rule. People who consider themselves the most advanced and most progressive have brought the earth to its most advanced state of peril. Peace, order, and good government do not characterize present civilization upon earth. Unity, interconnectedness, interrelatedness, and other assumptions about the universe stemming from the theory of Tsawalk suggest that the prevailing assumptions of Western civilization may be incomplete.

What are these Western assumptions? One is that the nature of the universe can be illuminated only by the human mind. This assumption is related to another: that those humans who told tales were unscientific and therefore could have no substantive and reliable knowledge about the nature of existence. Legends, myths, and origin stories belong to a "primitive" phase of human evolution.

But whereas the theory of evolution holds that life evolved from simple to complex, from primitive species to more advanced species, the theory I present in this book holds, in keeping with traditional origin stories, that life did not evolve but began as complexity. Biological activity is not only secondary but also subject to the powers of the more primary processes of the spiritual realm.

That the universe is unified, interconnected, and interrelated are assumptions about both the physical and metaphysical realms found in Nuu-chah-nulth origin stories. In the first four chapters of this book I analyze Nuu-chah-nulth origin stories in an attempt to show how they provide insight into lived experience that simultaneously places human existence in both the physical and metaphysical realms. Chapter 5 examines Nuu-chah-nulth methods of knowledge acquisition – that is, methods of accessing the spiritual realm – as an alternative to scientific methodologies. Chapter 6 discusses traditional ceremonies and practices that complement the meaning of the origin stories and knowledge acquired. In the final chapter I articulate the theory of Tsawalk, which has implications for today. The theory suggests that while the human mind is necessary for human cognition and for accessing and acquiring information, it can also be a conduit for spiritual information that can complement or complete or further illuminate our understanding of existence.

Nuu-chah-nulth Words

The Nuu-chah-nulth words in this book are spelled roughly according to the Ahousaht accent. Accents can differ considerably among the fourteen Nuu-chah-nulth communities, which can cause confusion about spelling. Various phonetic systems, such as the international phonetic system and others, are not readable without training, and consequently I have avoided using them. The Nuu-chah-nulth words in this book should not be used for study of the language. Note that each chapter employs the Nuu-chah-nulth numbering system. The numbers are translated as follows.

Tsawalk	Chapter 1
Utla	Chapter 2
Xaats-sta	Chapter 3
Muu	Chapter 4
Suh-tcha	Chapter 5
Nuu-pooh	Chapter 6
Utl-pooh	Chapter 7

Most of the other Nuu-chah-nulth words used in the text are explained. *Oosumich* and *tloo-qua-nah* are used according to my own understanding since my first language is Nuu-chah-nulth. In some cases, the meaning can be inferred from the context. For example, the name Aulth-ma-quus is not interpreted, but the meaning is directly connected to the actual events of the story in which it is found.

Tsawalk

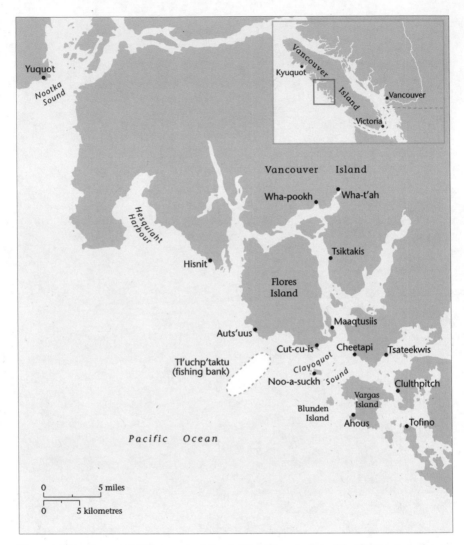

The northwest coast of Vancouver Island. The Nuu-chah-nulth placenames shown here are but a small sampling of the numerous places (seasonal community places, points of land, significant reefs, bays, rivers, lakes, and fish banks) that marked the sovereign territories of each Nuu-chah-nulth nation in precontact times.

1 TSAWALK

Origin Tales and the Nature of Reality: How Son of Raven Captured the Day

On the west side of Vancouver Island in British Columbia, Canada, are those who now call themselves Nuu-chah-nulth (people who dwell along the mountains). Historians and anthropologists referred to them as the Nootka Indians because Captain Cook misunderstood the local natives. According to oral history, the Mowachaht, who have lived in Nootka Sound for millennia, found Captain Cook apparently lost in a fog just outside of Friendly Cove. Since English was not yet a locally required language, they provided him the directions to safe harbour in the Nuu-chah-nulth language. The Nuu-chah-nulth phrase employed for the occasion, *nutkh-she-ee,* which sounds a little like "noot-ka" when shouted from a distance over the sea, means "to turn around." As the phrase gives no indication of direction, one can imagine that it was accompanied by a chorus of arms waving in large circles to indicate the route.

Fortunately, since then communication has improved between the two worlds to the point where a little understanding is now possible. Indeed, I hope that the presentation of a select few origin stories translated from the original Nuu-chah-nulth language might contribute to, and increase, the level of mutual understanding. Although, for the purpose of comparative analysis, it is necessary to bring Western perspectives into the discussion, the primary orientation of this book is toward the presentation of some important elements of a Nuu-chah-nulth worldview that may complement other knowledge systems.

Nuu-chah-nulth origin stories were typically told in family settings. Who today can appreciate the quality of those story settings during precontact times? Nuu-chah-nulth traditional houses are known in English as big, rather than long, houses. They could be as large as 40 feet by 100 feet in size, holding several nuclear families that belonged to one extended family. Without the noise of modern technology, inside

Quatsino village site. An example of traditional Nuu-chah-nulth housing on the West Coast of Vancouver Island in British Columbia, c.1866. *RBCM PN4649*

or outside the big house, the family gathered around the warmth of ancient fires undisturbed during long winter evenings. Each fire was connected endlessly to ancestral fires that were connected to the original fires from Qua-ootz, Owner of Reality. Each story was also connected to ancestral storytellers who had heard the story from the original storytellers.

Why is it that the setting of, or background to, each story was never told? Why is it that each story began at its most interesting point? "They had no light in the beginning. It was Son of Raven who ..." At each point of entry into a story the listeners become lost in their own creative imaginations about the awesome state of beginnings. With family gathered around, the fires are warm and inviting, and the light from the fire is a welcome reminder about the happy ending to the story. Son of Raven did bring the light into the world. But out beyond the family fires of the night is the darkness of the beginnings, and the presence of both fire and darkness means that the story itself is still alive. That is one reason why the setting of the story does not need to be explained. The storytellers and listeners gathered around the fires make up the setting. Their ancestors who passed on the stories provide the background, and in generations to come the listeners, too, will add to this background.

The setting of a story requires no introduction also because each story takes place in home territory. Mountains, rivers, lakes, streams, channels, islands, reefs, beaches, rocky bluffs, grassy flatlands, and the great ocean beyond are all familiar to each ear. Any of these areas might be the site of important historical or mythical events. Wherever one travels, one can be confronted by geographical landmarks associated with great events that provide orientation to, and an explanation of, the nature of existence. Each story was a story about home.

The nature of language in context is another reason that stories could begin without the need to explain the setting or background. The Nuu-chah-nulth language is what is known as a high-context language. Each Nuu-chah-nulth word may be associated with a world, or cultural and historical context, that is commonly understood. When Son of Raven, or anyone else speaks in a story, the Nuu-chah-nulth listener will automatically place that speech into a familiar cultural context of conditions. Unless otherwise stated or implied by the storyteller, the speaker in a story will be assumed to be addressing a group. Similarly, if the story takes place at Tsiktakis, it is not necessary to say that it is winter because every listener understands Tsiktakis to be a winter home. Common assumptions and understandings about meaning in a language that is connected to origins, to creation, to home territory, and to that territory's every life form demand little clarification.

English, on the other hand, is a low-context language. This may be the case mainly because it not only has been stripped of its original cultural context, but has accrued to itself words, such as "potlatch" and "Ottawa," from other languages. "Potlatch" originates from the Nuu-chah-nulth verb *pachitle* (to give). In English the word "potlatch" has been ascribed meanings associated with various institutions – social, economic, political – of the Western world. There is no generic equivalent to the English word "potlatch" in Nuu-chah-nulth. Not only is "potlatch" not a Nuu-chah-nulth word; it also has become a general classification that refers to every ceremonial form of feasting. Therefore, if it is said that someone gave a potlatch, it cannot be deduced from this statement whether the ceremony was a *tloo-qua-nah*, a *yax-ma-thlit*, a memorial, a rite of passage, a celebration of life, a marriage, an adoption, or a transfer of a chieftainship seat. During precontact times each ceremonial occasion had a very specific name that left no doubt about its purpose and meaning.

Consequently, there could be no ambiguity of meaning to the story as the family gathered around the warmth of those ancestral fires. The evenings themselves could become an eternity that was not only time-less, unhurried, and nonlinear, but also spatially motionless. While the storyteller and listeners experienced life without time in their physical bodies, their imaginations engaged with the action found in each story. There is wonder and magic in stories that tell of the exploits and foibles of animal characters. There can be no resistance to lessons found in them because they are indirect. Little boys or girls are not the apparent subjects or objects of lesson. It is Son of Raven who blunders through life. It is Son of Raven who captures the light of day. It is Son of Mucus who rescues the children. It is Crane who wants to marry Sawbill. It is Crane who floods the world.

Although the characters never change, a family would have its own version of a story. Despite variations of detail, however, common themes tended to remain intact, and the variations took nothing away from the principal truths conveyed. Therefore, the general verity of these stories cannot be found in word-for-word authenticity but in the commonal-ity of themes conveyed by the same stories from different families. For example, Nuu-chah-nulth stories about Son of Raven may be approached from any number of thematic perspectives. In the story where Son of Raven attempts, and quite humorously fails, to emulate Eagle's spec-tacular fishing strategy, the common theme is to teach that one should be oneself and not try to become like another. Some, or even many, of the details of this story may differ from one family to another, but the teaching about being true to oneself remains the same. According to Richard Erdoes and Alfonso Ortiz in *American Indian Trickster Tales*, "of all the characters in myths and legends told around the world through the centuries – courageous heroes, scary monsters, rapturous virgins – it's the Trickster who provides the real spark in the action – always hun-gry for another meal swiped from someone else's kitchen, always ready to lure someone else's wife into bed, always trying to get something for nothing, shifting shapes (and even sex), getting caught in the act, ever scheming, never remorseful" (Erdoes and Ortiz 1998, xiii).

The Nuu-chah-nulth, too, have stories that cover the entire range of life themes suggested by Erdoes and Ortiz, from heroic to loser and sub-lime to ridiculous, the timeless stuff of human experience. The stories selected for this volume were collected in the original language from the house of my grandmother Margaret Atleo in 1972. Unlike other stories about Son of Raven that might focus primarily upon foibles cre-ated by characteristics of personality such as greed, envy, an inflated ego, and covetousness, these stories focus more upon the grand themes of life. Who owns the light of day? Did someone transform the original beings into the life forms that are currently described as comprising biodiversity? Is marriage of divine origin or of human origin? Since there is great evil in the world capable of overwhelming the beings of earth, is there help available? These and other questions are answered through origin stories and consequently provide an orientation to life and reality that, prior to the onset of colonialism, allowed the Nuu-chah-nulth to manage their lives and communities for millennia.

Since it is assumed that origin stories contain elements of important truths about creation, it may be useful to ask how these ancient peoples discovered them without the aid of science? Is it possible that there are other ways to access truths about existence other than through science? These questions can be either misleading or useful depending upon the context – misleading in the context of science since science does not, perhaps cannot, recognize the verity of any truth outside its own self-imposed boundaries. However, the questions may be useful in the context of origin stories. Heretofore, scientific truth has been constrained by evidence founded in the context of a physical world. In contrast, spiritual truth is based on evidence founded in a spiritual context. Rules of evidence in one context do not necessarily apply to rules of evidence in another. For example, according to one common saying in the English language, a leopard cannot change its spots. This seems to be true in the physical world. However, in the spiritual world, transformation from one outward manifestation to another is commonplace. Thus Son of Raven and Son of Deer can change into a salmon and a salmonberry shoot respectively and back again into Son of Raven and Son of Deer. In this context, then, not only can a leopard change its spots, but it can also change its outward appearance completely.

Among the Nuu-chah-nulth, important truths about the nature of the universe are reflected in origin stories. In Western literature Son of Raven is known as a Trickster, and it is true that in many stories Son of Raven loves to play tricks, take advantage of people, take the easy way through life, and present a larger-than-life image to the world, but in the worldview of the Nuu-chah-nulth, Son of Raven is also much more than this. Son of Raven is also an archetype, a hero, and consequently yearns to do great deeds. However, in the process of attempting great deeds, Son of Raven, from the vantage point of earth, encounters problems, the solutions to which are naturally sought through, and from, the spiritual realm.

In the origin stories presented here the first story is about Son of Raven. This is then followed by three other origin stories about Aint-tin-mit (Son of Mucus). Aint-tin-mit first destroys an evil giant, then goes to his

Son of Raven, who helped the first people by bringing light into the world.
Illustration by Cleesemeek

spiritual home in the heavens to get married, and finally returns to earth to create biodiversity. Each of these stories is then followed by an analytic commentary that explains the Nuu-chah-nulth perspective about the human condition and nature of existence suggested by these stories.

HOW SON OF RAVEN CAPTURED THE DAY

They had no light in the beginning. Son of Raven suggested that they try to capture the day. Across the waters a Chief[1] owned the light of day, which he kept carefully guarded in a box. The people who lived in darkness grew tired of this and wondered what to do.

"How can we do that?" he was asked.

"We will entertain the Chief with a dance. Son of Deer, who can not only run fast but also leap far, will dance. If we are to capture the day, Deer must dance as one who is inspired, as one who captivates an audience."

"And then what will happen?" they asked Son of Raven.

"Deer will have soft dry cedar bark tied behind him. When no one seems to expect it, he will dance close to the day box and dip this bark into the fire."

"Yes, that's a good idea!" they said.

[In order for Son of Deer to dance for the Chief who owned the day, protocols had to be observed. Petitions, preparations, prayers, cleansing ceremonies, and a great deal of self-discipline and practice would take place before Son of Deer could appear before the Chief. These protocols do not appear in the story because every listener during traditional times would have been well versed in the necessity of observing appropriate diplomatic processes. In fact, an important underlying assumption about traditional experience is that the whole of life and existence is characterized by relationships that are inherent.]

All was now prepared. Every exacting detail of ritual, ceremony, and practice had been observed. Son of Deer was dressed in his finest dancing costume, and the soft dry cedar bark was now carefully tied behind him. When they reached the other side, the dancing began.

The Chief and his people watched. At first there was little evident interest in the dancing. This is usual. Highly accomplished people are not easily impressed. But gradually Son of Deer's dancing began to take hold of his audience. He danced with inspiration fuelled by the desire to fulfill a great need. He danced tirelessly, effortlessly, drawing strength from all those who lived in darkness. Now he danced by the day box. Without missing a beat he dipped the dry cedar bark into the day box. Instantly it caught fire and Son of Deer sprang for the door. But the Chief and the people were quicker. Before Son of Deer could leap out of reach, the fire was snuffed out. Now the Chief and his people knew that Son of Raven wanted the daylight. From now on the day box would be more closely guarded.

The people who lived in darkness regrouped.

"Go and get Wren, the wise one," Son of Raven said. When Wren arrived he offered the following advice: "The Chief has two beautiful daughters, and the sockeye salmon are running now. Women will be cleaning and preparing fish. Turn yourselves into sockeye and swim to the other shore. When you are captured you will then have an opportunity to kidnap the Chief's daughters."

So everyone transformed into sockeye, except Son of Raven, who would be satisfied with nothing less than taking the form of a giant king salmon. When the people of the day saw the huge king salmon they asked, "Is it not Son of Raven? Yes, it must be he who wishes to take the day from us." When Wren subsequently advised a transformation into salmonberry shoots, which were also then in season, Son of Raven again foiled the plan with egotistical one-upmanship by transforming into a giant salmonberry shoot.

However, Wren is not named "he who always speaks rightly" without good reason. Rather than rejecting or chastising Son of Raven for his blunders, Wren devised a plan that would take advantage of Son of Raven's great desire to do great deeds. This new plan required that Son of Raven transform into a tiny leaf that would float in the Chief's well. When the Chief's daughter came for a drink, Son of Raven would manoeuvre himself in such a way that she would be made to swallow him.

So it happened that Son of Raven became a tiny leaf floating in the Chief's well. When the Chief's daughter came for a drink, she dipped her cup into the well. As she lifted her cup to drink, she blew the tiny leaves away from her side of the cup. She drank deeply. One tiny leaf drifted toward her mouth. Before she could stop, she had swallowed it.

"Oh well, it's only a leaf," she thought.

But not long after this, the daughter became pregnant. She wondered how it could have happened, for she had no husband. In due time she bore a son. It was a crybaby. It cried so much that the mother and her relatives were all suspicious.

"Is it not Son of Raven?" the old people asked. "It seems to cry too much to be one of us."

But what if they were mistaken? What if the baby really belonged to the Chief's daughter? They could not be sure. So the baby was accepted.

As the baby grew, it continued to cry and whine a lot. When the baby was old enough, he loved to play in the canoes. All day he would play in these canoes. He also knew about the paddle of great power owned by his mother. With one stroke the paddle could propel any canoe a great distance. The boy began to whine for this paddle. He whined and whined. Finally his mother relented. Still the mother was careful. The boy could play with the paddle, but the canoe must remain tied to the shore. Again the boy whined and wheedled until he was allowed to paddle freely about. The boy was carefully watched, but nothing unusual happened. Gradually, the family began to trust him. Wasn't he just a boy who liked to play like other boys?

One day the boy began to play with the Day Box that sat in its usual well-guarded place. He wanted the Day Box to play with in his canoe, he said. The Chief would not hear of it. No, the boy must not play with the Day Box in his canoe. The boy pleaded. He cried. Over and over he wailed, "I want to play with the Day Box in my canoe! I want to play with the Day Box in my canoe! I want to play with the Day Box in my canoe!" He got on everyone's nerves. Day after day it was the same thing. "I want to play with the Day Box in my canoe!" Finally, the grandmother, in exasperation, told the boy's mother, "You never have mercy on him. Let him play with the Day Box in his canoe."

With the Day Box in his canoe, the boy was especially careful since he was closely watched. However, the boy did nothing unusual. He appeared content and happy simply to have the Day Box in his canoe while he played. Grandmother was happy. Mother was happy. The incessant crying and whining had stopped.

Meanwhile, among those who lived in darkness, Wren had sent some mice on an important mission across the waters to the shores of the Chief who owned the light of day. During the night the mice ate holes in all of the canoes except the one belonging to the boy. The next morning the boy began to play with the Day Box again. He was being watched but not so closely anymore. Then, all of a sudden, the boy gave a mighty thrust of his mother's paddle. Swiftly his canoe raced over the water toward the other shore. The Chief and his people panicked. They scrambled for their canoes. One by one, as the canoes were launched into the deep, they sank. The mice had done a good job.

As the boy neared the other shore, he began to uncover the Day Box very slowly. Now, for the first time, the people of darkness began to experience daylight. They looked and saw that it was Son of Raven who was coming to bring them the light. It grew brighter and brighter until the fullness of day was upon them.

Today, when the tide is out, you may notice that Son of Raven is the first to enjoy any food that is found at water's edge. That is his right and privilege, recognized by all Nuu-chah-nulth.

The Unity of the Physical and Spiritual

It is a characteristic of Nuu-chah-nulth origin stories that their teachings about life are implicit rather than explicit. The first sentence of this story, "They had no light in the beginning," does not differentiate between the physical and spiritual worlds because, unlike the contemporary division between the two, the Nuu-chah-nulth saw the physical world as a manifestation of the spiritual. More important, for all life forms, the two worlds were experientially one, which is the meaning of the Nuu-chah-nulth phrase *heshook-ish tsawalk* (everything is one). Nevertheless, it is assumed that the Creator creates the physical world from the spiritual. Son of Raven's physical body is transformed with relative ease into other kinds of physical bodies, such as a salmon, a salmonberry shoot, a tiny leaf, and the child of the Chief's daughter, but in all cases the essential being-hood of Son of Raven remains the same. One can infer from his name that, in the beginning, physical beings originated from the spiritual realm. The first raven is a son, and since the original source of life is Qua-ootz, this can only mean that Son of Raven experienced a spiritual birth just as all other beings, such as Son of Deer, are first created from the spiritual realm.

Clearly indicated in the story is that communication and travel between the physical and spiritual worlds were not unusual. The usage of the past tense, *were*, does not necessarily indicate that the time of communication and travel between the two worlds is over or no longer possible; it simply means that this activity may not be as common today as it was in the precontact past. In one sense, this story about Son of Raven is completely concerned with communication and travel between the physical and spiritual worlds. The *waters* are a metaphor that indicates not only the degree of difficulty in communication and travel, but also the substantive connection between the two realms. Since all Nuu-chah-nulth hold that the means to spiritual communication must be kept secret, this activity does not appear in the story. This spiritual activity is not for the public ear, and is therefore left as an unspoken assumption. Everyone knew that no one ever embarked upon a great exploit without spending a great deal of time in preparation, prayer, fasting, cleansing – occasionally, for months at a time – until an assurance or a sign was received that the great exploit could be successful.

The Human Condition
At one time the people of earth lived in darkness, and there was a need for light. Implicitly, then, the story teaches that in the physical realm darkness preceded light, for wherever light travels it is preceded by darkness. Another implicit teaching is that people have a natural desire for light and a natural antipathy toward darkness. Light is associated with life, knowledge, and wisdom, while darkness is associated with death, ignorance, and evil. This natural desire for light lies at the heart and core of Son of Raven, the archetype.

In this desire for light there is also evident a natural desire to do great deeds. The desire for heroic exploits is a natural condition of human existence. Heroic exploits can be public and widely acclaimed or virtually shrouded in secrecy. Irrespective of whether it is accomplished in public or in private, greatness is a natural human desire. Son of Raven aspired to greatness, and he succeeded. However, Son of Raven also failed more times than he succeeded, and this is another teaching about the human condition.

Although humans naturally desire light, and naturally desire to do great deeds, there is a problem with the human ego. It seems that human egos are easily overly inflated. Whenever Son of Raven transforms himself, and blunders under the influence of an overly inflated ego, it is often to the merriment of story listeners. He becomes, quite comically, a giant king salmon rather than the smaller sockeye salmon and creates a bizarre image that is so obvious to the other community that the strategy fails. At the same time it is useful to remember that although Son of Raven's blunders create a comic effect, these are acts of real power. Son of Raven has never gone away or become extinct. His capacity for blunder and transformative power remain to this day. Don't they?

Community as a Natural State

There is an assumption in the story that community is a natural phenomenon. Although ideas may originate in one person, it is the community members who come together to act in concert about common causes. Son of Raven articulates the idea to capture the day, but everyone automatically becomes involved. Everyone becomes a salmon. Everyone cooperates, and the community acts like a team. Interdependence is taken for granted. A specific Nuu-chah-nulth teaching associated with the idea of community is that if one doesn't ask for help when help is needed, then one is not friendly, one is not kind. One is not *aphey*. Among Nuu-chah-nulth, a very strong teaching is an admonition to be kind, or *aphey*. One of the strongest criticisms of another person's character is to say, "that person is not *aphey*." Consequently, a person in need is taught and encouraged to depend upon neighbours, and this interdependence is considered one of the strengths of a traditional Nuu-chah-nulth community.

When the first plan to capture the day fails, there is no question about perseverance and endurance. Work, perseverance, and endurance are unquestioned qualities in the story. No one complains about participating in the plan to capture the day. No one says that they've got other things to do, that they're not up to it right now, or that they've got a sore back. There are other Nuu-chah-nulth stories about what happens to people who don't like to work. While hardworking people are admired and held in esteem, lazy people are considered liabilities, and if laziness persists they can be expelled from the community.

There is also a ready acceptance of roles. There is no grumbling about what a misfortune it is to be slim and fast, like Son of Deer, which is why Son of Deer is chosen to execute the first plan. Son of Deer is not only slim and fast, but also a graceful dancer. No one can quite float through the air as gracefully as Son of Deer or move with such ease. Wren accepts the role of a wise person but not in an authoritative sense.

Wren does not presume to develop all community plans but waits, in this case, until invited before making a contribution.

Implicit in the story is the necessity of one's developing and growing in order to acquire knowledge and new skills. The first plans fail because of the intervention of egotism. A swelled-head approach to resolving the problems of life does not seem to be very effective. Twice Son of Raven presumes to become greater than everyone else, and twice Son of Raven foils the plan because of his swollen self-pride, because of an inaccurate self-perception. Today these experiences would be called "on-the-job training."

This type of knowledge acquisition and skill development is necessary for any initiative that has never been attempted before. Scientists searching for new areas of knowledge are quite familiar with this approach. A scientific theory is developed, tested, reformulated, and tested again until a good fit is found between theory and outcome. In the same way, different kinds of spiritual communication patterns may be developed and tested until a good fit is found between a particular prayer pattern and a particular need. Son of Raven's comic blunders can metaphorically describe communication patterns between the physical and spiritual realms that do not succeed. Human skill, such as the graceful dance of Son of Deer, or human ego, such as that exhibited by Son of Raven, are ineffective models of communication between the spiritual and physical realms. That a trial and error process to discover an appropriate communication pattern was necessary indicates a natural condition of growth, knowledge acquisition, and skill development.

Yet despite several mistakes Wren does not take Son of Raven to task. Wren does not question Son of Raven's authenticity as a genetically complete being or question his inherent capability to accomplish great deeds. Genetic evolution is unknown to Wren. Son of Raven is a completed creation, and it is Wren's role, as a wise person, to devise an appropriate plan for Son of Raven to execute successfully. Eventually, after much patience and perseverance, Wren fulfills his role, coming up with an appropriate plan that provides a model for achieving effective communication and ultimately greatness. Son of Raven must assume the role of a tiny insignificant leaf floating in a spring well. Son of Raven must become so tiny that if he is swallowed he will barely be noticed. Instead of being the greatest, he must become the least. He must become an apparently harmless disposable. The road to effective communication and greatness, in this story, includes both the thought and act of humility.

There are many examples of this truism in Nuu-chah-nulth life. In the great Nuu-chah-nulth ceremonies of the past, a great chief always had a speaker. The important role of the speaker was to communicate the extent of his chief's *hahuulthi* (ancestral territory) and the greatness of his lineage because it was taught that one did not engage in personal boasting about oneself. This Nuu-chah-nulth teaching is derived directly from origin stories such as this one about Son of Raven. This teaching included parents' regard for their children. One did not boast to others about the greatness of one's children. As an uncle explained to me: "We let others do that."

In this story there are several values that become evident in the telling. In addition to the personal values already mentioned – a work ethic, perseverance, endurance, patience, kindness, a desire for light and greatness – there are also relational values. The first of these relational values might be called helpfulness to the common good. Both Son of Raven and the community are willing to be helpful for the common good. This value is a constant family teaching, *hupee-ee-aulth* (be helpful). The teaching about being helpful to others is a pragmatic admonition designed to fit observed reality, to fit the nature of existence. In this sense, the value of helpfulness is a call to cooperate with the original design of creation, which is characterized by oneness, wholeness, interconnectedness, and interrelationality. The antithesis of helpfulness is contrary to creation.

A person who is not helpful in an appropriate context makes life more difficult. During precontact times, people often required help with their heavy wooden canoes. It was often necessary for people to go out in their canoes to forage for seafood, such as mussels, clams, gooseneck barnacles, sea urchins, abalone, and the like. The best time for this important activity is during low tide, which meant that they often arrived home during midtide. In order to protect their canoes from the constant pounding of ocean waves, it was always necessary to pull each canoe above the high-tide mark. Since it is not easy for community members to discern when anyone on the beach might require help, it was perfectly logical to require that the *forager* assume the responsibility of asking for help. Quite naturally each person who responded to the call for help also had a right to a share of the seafood that had been brought in.

A closely related value is generosity, which also derives from the instruction to be *aphey* (kind). To be *aphey* included not only greeting another with a happy smile and a handshake, but also the act of being generous. Thus if visitors are not invited to eat during mealtimes, it is considered *wiikhey* (an unkind act). The reverse is also true. Unless a visitor has already eaten, it is an unkind act to refuse a meal when invited. In an archetypal sense, Son of Raven is instrumental in giving a vital gift of light. In a metaphorical sense, one key characteristic of creation is that it is constantly giving of its light. If light is not a constant gift, life is not possible. Giving is natural to creation – in effect, a law of life. Giving can also be perceived from a cyclical perspective of modern science. The heavens give rain to the mountains and earth, which give water to the rivers and streams, which fill the oceans, which return the water in the form of vapour to the heavens. The interdependence and interrelationships of the natural world reflect the interdependence and interrelationships of all life forms.

Finally, there are two relational values that form the core and heart of the Nuu-chah-nulth way: love and respect. Little of love can be described on the printed page, but its active ingredients are an experience of the heart, of one's soul and life essence. The family setting for storytelling might include the warmth of a winter night's fire, the closeness of loved ones, warm tones of voice, feelings of security, familiar facial expressions, the imaginative gesticulations that evoke mental images, the absolute confidence of little ones in their families, and altogether these bring home some of the meaning of love. The word is not used in the story, but the story itself is a story of love. One of our own, with community involvement, brings home the light. Everyone has helped. It's a funny, beautiful story. It has a great ending.

However, in the Nuu-chah-nulth language, the word for love, *yaw-uk-miss*, includes the experience of pain. The Nuu-chah-nulth experience over millennia has found the goodness of love to be inseparable from the experience of pain. *Yaw-uk-miss* can be seen more clearly in the saga of Aint-tin-mit (Son of Mucus), a story recounted in the next chapter.

Respect is defined by Webster's dictionary as "the special esteem or consideration in which one holds another person or thing." While respect can easily include all people, this dictionary definition is very exclusive. People who tend to be held in *special* esteem by others might be the highest achievers and those considered the most outstanding in their field. Or, in the case of family favourites, one may be held in special esteem by a parent; in the case of schooling, another may be held in special esteem by a teacher. The point here is that the majority of the population in general must live without this special esteem. By comparison, the Nuu-chah-nulth word *isaak* (respect) necessitates a consciousness that all creation has a common origin, and for this reason *isaak* is extended to all life forms. The mystery of creation has created a network of relationships characterized by *isaak*.

However, in the Nuu-chah-nulth culture, *isaak* is not understood in humanistic terms and is therefore difficult to uphold and maintain on a daily basis. *Isaak* is not a concept of human origin but is understood in terms of creation. *Isaak* in practice guides one toward an understanding of creation and its meaning. It creates a climate or environment for the practitioner in which communication with other life forms is possible. It made effective communication between the Nuu-chah-nulth and animals like the salmon and wolf a reality. It is a very simple idea.

This perspective about the nature of relationships between all life forms in creation has been called a worldview. Even Nuu-chah-nulth words can emphasize the underlying unity of creation. For example, the word for grandchild is *qua-ootz*, the same word that Chief Maquinna gave to the Spanish explorer José Mariano Moziño when asked for the Nuu-chah-nulth word for God. The word literally means "owner (*ootz*) of reality (*qua*)." Plays on words, and even plays on stories, are not unusual in Nuu-chah-nulth culture. The Nuu-chah-nulth name for grandchild is a permanent reminder that life is a gift and that all creation belongs to Qua-ootz. It is the recognition that although humans procreate, Qua-ootz is the Creator. Since the Creator owns everything, all must be held in esteem. Thus it is said that *isaak* is not of human origin. *Isaak* in this context can be understood as a pragmatic stance in keeping with creation's original design of wholeness.

Consequently, in the story of Son of Raven, it makes complete sense to interpret the relationship between the characters as respectful. Wren does not take Son of Raven to task because Wren can see and understand Son of Raven as a creation of Qua-ootz. Son of Raven is a completed being and deserves to be respected. There is no suggestion of an evolutionary creation wherein some species are more advanced than other species on some imaginary scale. It might be argued that Son of Raven does not respect Wren because Son of Raven modifies Wren's plans. This is true and presents a lesson about what not to do in life. When Son of Raven's *esteem for himself* becomes *too special* – that is, when Son of Raven becomes too proud, when he allows his ego to become overly inflated – an imbalance with other egos is created. This imbalance leads to Son of Raven's disrespectful act, which is to alter Wren's plan. It seems that from the very beginning, Son of Raven has provided a very accurate reflection of the human condition.

Assumptions about the Nature of Reality: *Heshook-ish Tsawalk*

Approached from the perspective of a Nuu-chah-nulth worldview, the story of Son of Raven provides a number of indications about the nature of reality. As indicated earlier, reality is perceived as a unity: *heshook-ish tsawalk*. The physical and spiritual realms are metaphorically connected and interrelated by the great *waters*. Although daylight is a physical manifestation emanating from stars, its origin is spiritual. Light comes from another world that is perceived to be the source of all creation, all existence. Son of Raven understood this principle of creation, and his role in life, in concert with his community, was to discover an appropriate method or strategy for interacting with the spiritual realm.

The exercise is somewhat like discovering the correct combination to the lock that opens a storehouse of life's necessities. This process can be compared to the scientific method of proposing a theory that is then tested for its degree of consonance with experience. The outcome of the tests may suggest an alteration or modification to the theory or that the proposed theory be abandoned altogether. In the same way, Son of Raven discovers through trial and error that some of his ideas do not fit the lock that unlocks the storehouse of life's necessities. Hence, although everything is one and thus in unity, there are laws of operation that must be discovered – which leads us to another characteristic of creation.

The universe is polyphasic or multidimensional to the empirical eye. In the beginning, Nuu-chah-nulth people did not differentiate between the spiritual and physical dimensions but simply assumed that interaction between the two realms was normal. It was well understood that all things come from the spiritual realm. One means of initiating a positive interaction with the spiritual realm is called *oosumich*. *Oosumich* is a secret and personal Nuu-chah-nulth spiritual activity that can involve varying degrees of fasting, cleansing, celibacy, prayer, and isolation for varying lengths of time depending upon the purpose. In order to establish an acceptable protocol with the spirit of a whale, my great-grandfather Keesta performed his spiritual ceremonies for eight months because the great personage of the whale demanded the *honour* of extended ceremony. For more common activities, such as fishing and hunting, one might *oosumich* for three or four days. Whatever powers or gifts were sought, the principle behind *oosumich* remained the same: that effective access to the spiritual dimension from the physical dimension was absolutely necessary. Such is the nature of creation, of existence.

There are many kinds of powers in the spiritual realm, some beneficial, some healing, some hurtful, some painful, and some even destructive to the point of causing death. The physical dimension is like a mirror or shadow of the spiritual realm. If the spiritual realm contains good powers, earth beings can experience good powers in the physical realm. If the spiritual realm contains destructive or negative powers, the same destructive or negative powers can be experienced in the physical realm. That the physical realm is like a mirror or shadow of the spiritual realm implies a special relationship.

The relationship between the spiritual and physical dimensions is characterized by the latter's dependence upon the former. Spiritual things do not derive from physical things, but physical things derive from the spiritual. For this reason, Son of Raven, together with his community, must travel across the great waters to capture the necessary light. Although earth beings are dependent upon the spiritual realm for existence, they are not apathetic in their relationship with the spiritual dimension, nor is the relationship necessarily marked by a superior-inferior distinction such that earth beings must respectfully petition and meekly await a mysterious largesse from the spiritual realm. The clue to the dynamic relationship between created beings and a spiritual Creator is the metaphor of Son of Raven becoming a tiny leaf and in so doing becoming a child of the Great Chief (Creator). It is possible, then, for beings to be born of the spirit again in order to access physical necessities. In this sense, the dependence of the physical upon the spiritual is much like the relationship between parents and dependent young people. Ordinarily young people not only enjoy the immediate benefits of being in a family, but also stand to inherit the wealth of their parents in the future. Since he had been born into the Chief's family, Son of Raven had natural birthrights to the benefits of this family.

It may be true that the possibility that people can become children of the Creator, as Son of Raven became a child of the Chief, remained a mystery to the Nuu-chah-nulth until Christianity brought a similar story. It had been thought that only Son of Raven could become the child of the Creator. The Christ figure is an archetype of the Creator's child. Follow this archetype or model, and the promise of Godly inheritance becomes a reality. The story of Son of Raven is also a story of archetypes. Son of Raven is an archetypal hero and saviour. Son of Raven brought the light into the Nuu-chah-nulth world just as Christ brought the light into the world.

However, as every Nuu-chah-nulth elder knows, Son of Raven is also an archetype of the foolish side of human nature. In other stories, Son of Raven likes to take the easy way through life, which always creates unanticipated problems. In one story previously alluded to, instead of devising an appropriate strategy of his own, Son of Raven decides to copy Eagle's fishing style. Eagle dives from a great height and swoops swiftly down upon an unsuspecting salmon. One requirement for this strategy, among others, is keen eyesight. All Nuu-chah-nulth people know that Son of Raven has very poor eyesight; as a consequence, he mistakes a dark reef in the water for a salmon, knocking himself unconscious, and floats away unceremoniously with his legs up in the air.

Another important archetype in the story of Son of Raven is Wren. Wren provides a model of the wise person. In translation, Wren's name, Ah-up-wha-eek, literally means "a condition of speaking wisely" and would likely be translated as "one who speaks the right words." At the beginning of this book is a narrative about my great-grandfather Keesta that may illustrate Wren as an archetype. Keesta's experience likely took place toward the end of the nineteenth century, and the narrative picks up the story where Wren intervenes: "Keesta took his knife, and as he moved to cut the rope, Ah-up-wha-eek (Wren) landed on the whale and spoke to Keesta: 'Tell the whale to go back to where it was harpooned.' Keesta spoke to the whale, and immediately the great whale turned according to the word of Wren, the little brown bird, and returned to where it was first harpooned, and there it died."

On this point, a Nuu-chah-nulth commentary might be translated as, "Wren must have *up-wha*" – that is, *spoken* the right words in the context of the situation. A typical response to this observation would be that "Wren must have *up-wha* because he *is* Ah-up-wha-eek." Wren speaks rightly and wisely because such speech is in Wren's nature, just as the archetypes of heroism and foolishness attributable to the Son of Raven reflect the heroic and foolish in human conduct.

Another typical Nuu-chah-nulth perspective on Keesta's experience with his wife, Wren, and the whale is that the hunt was meant to happen that way. In other words, there was a reason for, or a purpose in, the design of events as they unfolded. Keesta's wife departed prematurely from her ceremonial position because she misunderstood the information received about the whale. She thought that the whale had been captured and killed and was in the process of being towed ashore. Keesta's wife made a mistake but not in the wrong spirit. She departed from her ceremonial position to prepare to welcome the whale and celebrate appropriately. Nevertheless, Keesta's wife might be said to have breached the agreement with the spirit of the whale achieved by Keesta during his ceremonial and spiritual preparation up in the mountains. Although the *letter* of the agreement may have been breached, the *spirit* of the agreement was not. That is, Keesta's wife went about her usual preparations for the whale in the right spirit. Since the spirit of the agreement remained intact, the breach of the letter of the law was overridden and the agreement with the whale was consummated. What then was the reason or purpose for all this high drama?

According to the Nuu-chah-nulth, existence is purposeful. One of the purposes of creation is for humans and Qua-ootz or other spiritual representatives to reach firm agreements. This purpose, which is confirmed by the Nuu-chah-nulth's experience, is emphasized when the terms of these agreements are disrupted. Keesta's wife inadvertently broke the terms of the agreement between the two realms, creating a momentary problem. If there had been no momentary problem, there might be sound reason to question the validity of the accepted pattern of relationship between the physical and spiritual realms. A successful whaling expedition might be attributed to happy coincidence rather than to a firm agreement reached after great struggle. Wren demonstrates the unity of the physical and spiritual realms by appearing strategically at the point when Keesta is about to cut loose the whale. Wren, the angelic emissary in this case, speaks authoritatively, Keesta obeys without hesitation, and the agreement is ultimately consummated.

Another purpose of creation suggested by the story of Keesta is to make possible the spiritual realm's expression of a measure of grace toward the physical realm – as is necessitated when humans commit unintended breaches of contract. Human frailty, arising from the finitude of being human, creates many unintended errors of judgment, such as the one made by Keesta's wife. In spite of this error of judgment, heaven intervened, so to speak, in the form of Wren, whose manifestation as a messenger is acceptable to both the Nuu-chah-nulth and the Creator, just as angelic forms are manifestations acceptable to other peoples and the Creator.

Another purpose of creation is to foster wholeness or community, for that is the natural order of existence. Wholeness is not an ideology like socialism or communism but the very essence of life. Nor is this purpose restricted to human communities: It applies to all created beings. Thus the traditional Nuu-chah-nulth paid respect to the arrival of the first salmon of the season by conducting a welcoming ceremony of recognition and thanksgiving. The salmon people have their own communities and purpose, and this purpose is related to all life forms, including people. Similarly, great ceremonies were conducted in recognition and acknowledgment of the life of a cedar tree that would soon be transformed into living tools, viable housing, and important transportation items.

A very commonplace observation at all times everywhere is that one of the characteristics of existence is struggle. Son of Raven accepted struggle as a necessity, as a given. Although there are numerous immediate comforts in life, such as water, air, and all the resources found within any ecosystem, the characteristics of existence are such that struggle, work, effort, training, preparation, practice, decision making, cooperation, skill development, and management are required to secure and maintain housing, community infrastructure, language, and cultural, individual, family, community, national, and global wholeness. Son of Raven and his community did not question this assumption about the condition of reality. To employ stereotypical phrases, they put on their "thinking caps" to plan, and "rolled up their sleeves" to execute each plan, and persevered, and did not give up until they were successful.

Their route to success is a classic means-end issue. Will the execution of any means justify an end, however good and beneficial that end may be? According to this story, the *means* must fit the *end*. Although a body of water connects the two realms within the story, and although everything is one, the two communities are nevertheless separate peoples within this unity of creation. Son of Raven is a member of one community that desires a resource or benefit that the other community controls. The resource or benefit is light. Every means utilized by Son of Raven to capture this resource fails while he is a member of his own community. It is not until Son of Raven is born into the Chief's community that his effort to capture the daylight succeeds.

Son of Raven acquires membership in this community, the rights of citizenship, and a birthright to the resources of the Chief. There is a direct relationship between membership in a community and the resources of that community. So long as Son of Raven did not have membership in the Chief's community, every *means* that he employed to capture the daylight was illegitimate, unsuitable, inappropriate, and unacceptable. Those born into a country have stronger and more deeply rooted ties to that country and its resources than those who acquire citizenship through immigration. Son of Raven was born into the community that owned the daylight and thereby gained direct access and rights to its benefits. Fortunately, Son of Raven retained membership within his original community as well, and thus they too came to enjoy these same benefits.

Finally, the story of the Son of Raven unveils the apparent superficiality of differences between life forms. Son of Raven at first shows himself to be an egotistical and vain fool, one who is constantly trying to socially place himself above his neighbours. He cannot, at first, see himself as equal to anyone else. He must be a giant king salmon rather than the smaller sockeye salmon. But Son of Raven is more than a fool; he also seeks greatness, which is the glorious aspect of vanity. Wren, the wise, completes Son of Raven, the fool, by providing a perfect means to greatness through an act of humility, which is an apparent contradiction to vanity.

The superficiality of differences is also unveiled by the appearance of each character. Today, Raven, Deer, Wren, Wolf, Bear, Eagle, and the host of life forms that make up biodiversity on earth have a common ancestry. The phrase "all my relations" refers to this common ancestry. Despite outward differences each life form depends upon the others for wholeness and completeness. The apparent differences between life forms are real but not in any essential way. Community is a natural order of existence, and one of its functions can be to reconcile the apparent differences perceived among its members.

He-xwa ◈ The Struggle for Balance

When people *he-xwa* they are said to be struggling with the tensions of life forces. It is not the ordinary struggle that might take place when a canoe or house is in need of minor repair. *He-xwa* refers to struggles that may tax to the limit every human resource. When the survival of a community is threatened, it is certainly an occasion for *he-xwa*. Sometimes, particularly when the outside force that threatens the survival of a community is greater than the collective resources available, it becomes necessary for an intervention by an otherworldly source. Such is the case in the story that follows.

Aint-tin-mit and Aulth-ma-quus (Son of Mucus and Pitch Woman)
This story of a Nuu-chah-nulth hero and rescuer comes from one of the families of the Ahousaht branch of the Nuu-chah-nulth. It is a story about the nature of good and evil as natural to existence, a story about the marriage between the physical and the spiritual, a story about a synergy between these two realms that is inherent to creation. It is also a story about upholding the natural relationship found in family and community, the maintenance of such bonds being one of the purposes of life; it is a story about *yaw-uk-miss,* the unity of love and pain, the place of willpower and manifest destiny, the nature of evil, the discipline of grieving, the legitimacy of state membership, and the issues of means and ends. Aint-tin-mit (Son of Mucus) is a Nuu-chah-nulth hero, rescuer, and transformer. Why did Aint-tin-mit, who had come from the place of spirits and subsequently returned to this same place of spirits, become *quus* (human)?

> One day while the people were living at Ahous,[1] the Chi~~~
> daughter went to play on the beach with the rest of th~

children. They had all been warned about Aulth-ma-quus, the ugly giant woman who stole children. They say she lived high up in the mountains, where she took all the abducted children. But children have no time to worry while at play. Every moment of play is filled with the keen enjoyment of life. It would be during such moments of play that Aulth-ma-quus, with a gigantic basket on her back, would come down the mountain chewing a great wad of gum. Aulth-ma-quus was very large, very strong, and very ugly. She was so large and so ugly that when children saw her, the tiniest ones would freeze in terror. Emanations from a powerful evil presence can be felt by spiritually sensitive little hearts, which are then gripped with terror.

It was such a day while the Chief's daughter played on the beach that Aulth-ma-quus appeared and began to scoop up the terror-stricken children with her large hands and throw them screaming into her basket. It was after this particular raid that one child who had been captured by Aulth-ma-quus managed to escape and find her way back home. She went to the Chief and told him that Aulth-ma-quus had taken all the children to her great house in the mountains. There she had put gum over all the children's eyes so that they could no longer see.

Now the people knew where their children had been taken. They wanted desperately to get their children back, but they were afraid of this ugly giant. They were afraid of her power and her strength. What were they to do? Who was able to rescue their beloved children? Who could restore family and community to wholeness? But no one in all the land was found who could rescue the children.

So it was that the Chief's wife grieved exceedingly for her daughter. She cut her hair as was the custom when mourning. She wept and wailed until her nose ran with mucus. She wiped her nose and flung the mucus away. She noticed that no matter how she flung her mucus it would land, as though guided, into one specific mussel shell. She continued her grieving but soon noticed that the mussel shell had begun to move. A modern woman would no doubt be startled, incredulous, and suspicious of anything so unnatural. Fortunately, she was a *hakum* (the wife of a chief), and as her tears continued to flow her heart filled with wonder at the tiny feet sticking out of the mussel shell. She dried her tears and went for a closer look. Today it would be called a miracle, but in those days it was not an unusual phenomenon. People were always transforming into salmon or leaves and other such beings. The mucus of the Chief's wife had transformed into a baby.

She took the baby to her husband and explained how it had been born. Her husband instructed her to take it to her aunt and uncle who were wise in the care of babies. The baby cried as other babies cry, but it did not grow in the ordinary way. No, the baby grew rapidly. He became a boy far sooner than ordinary babies did. All the people were amazed. Especially since they knew that the Chief's wife had not been pregnant. Yet they marvelled at the manner of birth and accordingly, as was the custom, named the child Aint-tin-mit (Son of Mucus).

As a boy, Aint-tin-mit was wise beyond his years. He was knowledgeable about all things and was skilful with his hands. Still, the Chief's wife continued to grieve for her stolen daughter. Occasionally, Aint-tin-mit would ask what she was sad about. Then, one day, it seemed right for the Chief's wife to tell Aint-tin-mit that her daughter had been stolen by Aulth-ma-quus.

At about this time, Aulth-ma-quus came again to steal children. Aint-tin-mit heard of the raid and was determined to do something about it. Of all the people, Aint-tin-mit alone did not fear this giant woman. So before setting off to rescue the children, Aint-tin-mit informed the people that they should post a lookout for his return.

Aint-tin-mit found the trail of the giant woman and followed it as silently as a shadow. After some time, he came to a great house in the mountains. Furtively he peered inside, and there he saw many children lined up against the walls. They sat in the same formation as that of people sitting at a great feast. They had gum over their eyes and thus had become blind.

As Aint-tin-mit pondered how to rescue the children, he noticed the giant woman leave her house to go to the spring well. Then he knew what to do. As the woman prepared to go again to the spring well, Aint-tin-mit ran to the well and climbed into an alder that overhung it. He took a position where the reflection of his face could be seen in the water. As the woman was dipping her water bucket into the spring well she noticed the reflection in the water.

"My, what a pretty woman I am!" she exclaimed. She paused for some time to admire the reflection. She experimented. First she smiled and sure enough the reflection smiled back at her. In turn, she grinned, laughed, and raised her eyebrows several times in quick succession. In turn, the reflection grinned, laughed, and raised its eyebrows several times in quick succession. How she admired that reflection in the pool!

Later, when the woman returned to the spring well again Aint-tin-mit confronted her with the truth.

"Oh!" she said, obviously disappointed. "And all this time I thought it was my own reflection. So it was yours. Tell me. How did you get to be so beautiful? Can you show me?"

"Of course!" Aint-tin-mit replied. "I can show you. Come with me." The woman followed.

Then Aint-tin-mit said, "Lie on that flat rock. Be sure to keep your eyes closed or it won't work. Lie still." Eagerly the woman lay down and closed her eyes. Then Aint-tin-mit picked up a large rock and prepared to crush the woman's head. But the woman's resolve wavered and three times she changed her mind and said, "No! No! No!"

The fourth time she changed her mind, Aint-tin-mit pretended to walk away until finally she said, "Okay! Let's do it!" With her eyes closed tightly shut the great rock came down and crushed her head. But something strange happened. Instead of blood, Aint-tin-mit saw that her head was made of gum. When she finally stopped struggling and lay still, he ran into her great house. There he noticed, hanging on a wall, a throbbing organ. It was Aulth-ma-quus's heart. He took out his bow and put an arrow into it.

To his surprise, a huge chamber pot became frantic and began yelling, "Ih-ih-kithla-mo-ka! Ih-ih-kithla-mo-ka! Ih-ih-kithla-mo-ka! A person has broken into your home!" In her own home, Aulth-ma-quus was known as Ih-ih-kithla-mo-ka. But Aint-tin-mit paid no mind because he knew that he had killed the woman. He wasted no time in gathering the children together. Being wise, he knew how to remove the gum from the children's eyes without hurting them. As he worked with the children, the chamber pot continued to yell for the giant woman. Finally, Aint-tin-mit smashed the chamber pot and kicked it outside. He went back to his work of rescue, but the chamber pot could still be heard protesting outside.

Finally, all the gum was removed, and the children blinked and squinted in the unfamiliar light of day. They were weak and undernourished, so Aint-tin-mit slowly and carefully led them down the mountain trail.

As they approached the village, the people's lookout saw the children. As news of the children's arrival spread, the village became a bustle of great activity and excitement. Mothers and fathers choked back their tears of joy and relief as they were reunited with their children. The Chief ordered a great feast. The people gathered together and ate heartily, sang for joy, and danced in thanksgiving. There they recognized Aint-tin-mit's achievement.

Family and Community

This origin story is about family and community as a natural state of existence. In the Nuu-chah-nulth worldview it is unnatural, and equivalent to death and destruction, for any person to be isolated from family or community. Nuu-chah-nulth life, therefore, is founded by creating and maintaining relationships. Ahous, the location of this story, was made up of several extended families that were interlinked through familial relationships. Each extended family lived in a big house. Each big house was, in turn, interrelated to every other big house in the community. Neighbouring communities were interrelated in the same way through marriage, such that it is still credible today to say that all Nuu-chah-nulth, from Neah Bay in Washington State to the most northern Nuu-chah-nulth community of Kyuquot, are related.

This origin story is also about evil and its destructive power as a natural state of existence. The Nuu-chah-nulth worldview, therefore, perceives that family and community must be maintained in the context of the ever-present reality of evil and the threat of its destructive force. Aulth-ma-quus is an archetypal person who represents this reality. While the design of creation is such that a family and community can handle most issues of life, such as the provision of food, clothing, shelter, medicine, entertainment, and governance, it sometimes happens that the strength of a community may be weakened enough to allow an evil force to dominate. Nuu-chah-nulth community strength is directly related to the practice and observance of teachings. When adherence to these teachings is prevalent, the community may be strong; when teachings are forgotten the community may become weak and find itself in trouble.

When the destructive forces of evil overcome a community to the point where it becomes broken, and if no earthly help is forthcoming, the unity of creation can become manifest. The *hakum* (chief's wife) is representative of this brokenness, and her mucus becomes the perfect medium for an immaculate conception, who becomes known, after the Nuu-chah-nulth custom of naming, as Aint-tin-mit (Son of Mucus). Evil is overcome and the children are restored to community. The unity of creation is revealed through the cooperative interrelation between heaven and earth that produces Aint-tin-mit, whose sole purpose, at this time, was to rescue the children and restore them to family and community.

Purpose in Life

If it is true, as this origin story suggests, that family and community are a natural state of existence, it is also true that one purpose of life is to live in family and community. The word for home or house is *muh-us,* which means a state or condition of biting into the earth. A Nuu-chah-nulth home did not just sit mutely on top of a piece of land but aggressively and tenaciously bit into and held onto its own turf. This stance affirmed that it was there to stay; it had put down its own roots, so to speak. *Muh-us* also implies that the maintenance of family and community require a determined effort. Good families and communities do not happen naturally but require sustained cooperation. The people in the home were collectively referred to as *sta-kumlth,* which early Nuu-chah-nulth informants translated into English as "bunch" for inquisitive anthropologists. Thus lineages may be seen as a *sta-kumlth* (bunch).

Keesta *sta-kumlth* would therefore be translated, in part, as "that Keesta bunch." A more complete translation of Keesta *sta-kumlth* would be "the lineage within the house of Keesta." Metaphorically, then, the inhabitants of each Nuu-chah-nulth home could be pictured, in their biological relationships, as a "bunch" of grapes or berries on a single branch. Each grape or berry could have been differentiated in size, shape, colour, and condition of growth from every other grape or berry, but they all belonged to the same branch. It could be that early Nuu-chah-nulth informants were making that pragmatic analogy between a grape or berry branch and the lineage-like branch that constituted the occupants of each big house. By extending this analogy between the grape or berry branch and house lineage, it can be seen that each Nuu-chah-nulth community was made up of a bush that might have had a dozen or more branches; each bush, moreover, might have shared a common ancestral seed that stretched back to the time of creation. Chiefs Maquinna, Keitlah, and Keesta resided over separate houses, but they all had the same ancestor.

The time of creation brings to mind Qua-ootz, Owner of Reality, Creator. As *qua-ootz* is also a common word for "grandchild," the little spirit that enters the baby in the womb comes from the Great Spirit. Every precious grandchild is a living, breathing, shouting, screaming, puking, messing, peeing, gurgling, smiling, cooing, cuddling reminder of the connection and relationship of all things to the Creator. These gifts of children to *quus* (humans) must be cared for according to the original design of creation. One of the most important teachings about this design of original creation is the importance of relationships. *Cla-ya-hoe-aulth-ee yakh-yew-itk:* Greet with joy, gladness, and enthusiasm those who are related to you. Why should we greet our relatives in such a manner? Why shouldn't we just ignore them, or why shouldn't we be neutral and just say "hi"? In the Nuu-chah-nulth worldview, each family has a direct connection to the Creator through the gifts of the grandchildren. All relatives are therefore gifts from Qua-ootz, the Creator. If Qua-ootz, the Creator of everything, Owner of Reality, were to personally hand you a gift, how might you react? The Nuu-chah-nulth were encouraged to react positively and enthusiastically with practical demonstrations of kindness and love; thus they sought to make their visiting relatives feel welcome by providing them with all the necessities of home life.

If home and community are perceived as natural to creation, only the quality of these relationships remains to be determined. One of the functions of family *hahuupa* (teachings) was to improve or maintain the quality of these relationships. The teaching that one should greet visiting relatives with joy and love emphasizes the great value of relatives who are closer and live in the same house. Young girls were known as *usma*, denoting the loved, the precious, the revered, the undefiled, the chaste (Clutesi 1969). In the story of Aint-tin-mit, the *hakum*'s daughter, who is stolen by Aulth-ma-quus, is *usma*. She is loved, she is precious, she is revered, she is undefiled, and she is chaste. This is the background to a set of family and community conditions that are violently disrupted, leading to family and community trauma.

Consequently, when a member of a family is lost, this state of loss is contrary to creation's original design. It is perhaps in this sense that Black Elk has said: "The chief proposition of the universe is relationality." A primary purpose in life is to create, maintain, and uphold relationships.

The Unity of Love and Pain

The story of Aint-tin-mit reflects the tension between loving relationships and a harsh reality that would destroy, devour, and annihilate these relationships. Aulth-ma-quus is an archetype of that harsh reality in which loving relationships must exist. It makes perfect sense, therefore, to incorporate the concept and experience of love and pain into one Nuu-chah-nulth word: *yaw-uk-miss*. In English *yaw-uk-miss* is translated as "love," but the etymology of the word clearly incorporates the experience of pain associated with danger. *Yaw-uk-miss* can also be translated as "pain." Love and pain exist quite naturally, without contradiction, as a unity of existence.

To say to someone *yaw-uk-up soo-wa* (I love you) is to mean more than the composite of love expressions found in human sex, human companionship, or human spirituality. *Yaw-uk-up soo-wa* may mean all of these things placed in the context of inherent danger, placed in the context of certainty that the joy of love is sharply defined by its opposites of pain or hatred. A precious baby is born into a world of love and joy, and this state of existence becomes all the more poignant when that baby is lost. If the brevity of life is perceived as a breath in winter, the bloom of a beautiful flower in spring, or the sudden appearance of a rainbow in fall, each can be defined as much by its presence as by its absence. Love, like life, is brief; while love is here it is a joy, but soon it is gone and there is grief. Love and pain are inseparable in the Nuu-chah-nulth worldview.

Willpower and Manifest Destiny

Yaw-uk-miss, as an experience in life, conforms to a pattern that creation affirms in this story. In practice, the experience of love in an environment of pain, or of pain in an environment of love, is neither chaotic nor without design. Although Aint-tin-mit experienced the best *hahuupa* (teachings) from the time of his birth, as was the custom in chiefly families, he always had the choice to accept or deny these teachings. The same would be true for Aulth-ma-quus. She, too, would have had an opportunity to accept or reject the teachings that she undoubtedly received in her family. The exercise of willpower concerning these teachings determines destiny. No two destinies can be identical. That is why, today, it is said that each family had its own teachings. Everyone has a place and purpose in life. Everyone has a role, and each place and purpose in life demands appropriate teachings for fulfillment. Each person can accept or deny the teachings of his or her own family. Consequently, each choice creates a design in life that may tend to create or tend to destroy. Aint-tin-mit and Aulth-ma-quus make clear choices as means to different ends. Both intend to live, but one intends to live through creation and the other through destruction.

Aulth-ma-quus and the Nature of Evil

It is not known if adult humans have ever seen Aulth-ma-quus. In a real sense it is not necessary to actually see Aulth-ma-quus any more than it is necessary to see the wind because the effects of both are everywhere. If you have ever lost a child to outside influences, you have "seen" Aulth-ma-quus. Children are forever being lured away from their homes by an Aulth-ma-quus effect. Once gone they become metaphorically blind to the truths of their former lives, as happens in this story. The gum that blinds the children's eyes is the same substance that defines Aulth-ma-quus's personhood. She is made of gum rather than flesh and blood. Everything that she represents becomes the social reality of the children. When children are lured completely into another environment, or way of life, they are influenced by that environment to the extent that they can see no other. Reality can be determined by what is set before the eyes.

The power to determine others' perceptions of reality, one expression of which today is known as advertising, was well known to the Nuu-chah-nulth through this origin story. Evil and destructive ways of life have the power to alter perception. In this case the evil is so great that the children are literally helpless to resist. They are trapped, imprisoned, and become totally blind to the goodness of their former community and way of life. This condition of existence led to many teachings that sought to ensure wholeness, health, and personal wellbeing. From the time of conception, a traditional Nuu-chah-nulth person was subject to a host of alternative influences, positive and negative, that were recognized and accepted as part of the natural state of creation.

The best form of influence came from parents and grandparents, who sought a good life for their progeny. This was done through a variety of customs and practical applications. The pregnant mother was taught to eat certain foods considered beneficial to her condition. She was not to be in the presence of angry people or to participate in funerals. In general she was admonished to avoid anything distasteful, dreadful, or deadly that might negatively influence the baby in her womb. These little teachings about how to approach life were taught as preventive measures in the context of the dangerous reality indicated by origin stories such as this one about Aint-tin-mit and Aulth-ma-quus. Life is lived in a context of danger that can be managed somewhat by the observance of sound teachings.

When the baby is born, the afterbirth is returned to the earth, together with symbols considered beneficial to a good and useful life. Thus, for the traditional Nuu-chah-nulth, the influences upon life do not begin at birth but in the womb. In that dark, warm place inside the mother, the teachings begin to influence and shape an identity. It is a process of orientation. Given that the life essence of the baby arrives from another place, the baby is completely disoriented – hence the necessity for the gentle and soothing orientation produced by constantly touching while singing to the baby. The lullaby songs are specifically about who the baby is and who and what the baby will become. The baby is small and tiny. The songs tell the baby that it is small and tiny. If the baby is to be a chief, the songs tell the baby that it will become a great chief. Alternatively, if the baby is to be an artist, or canoe maker, or artisan, or orator, or policeperson, or educator, or singer, or carpenter, or electrician, or prime minister, or chief justice, the songs will be about that promise.

The Discipline of Grieving

Grieving during traditional precontact times was not a simple matter of expressing sad feelings. Grieving was much more than an emotional experience. There were teachings and formalities that engaged the human will and intelligence. It is no accident that the one who grieves exceedingly in the story is a *hakum* (chief's wife). She is an actual human being, but she also represents a type of spiritual principle. Both the chief and his wife are archetypes of a spiritual pattern. Both *hawilth* (chief) and *hakum* (queen) denote power, authority, wealth, wisdom, generosity, excellence, and all the attributes of a divine being. A sacred role of the *hakum* in this case is to be a type of priestess who intercedes for her people through grieving.

Although she is representative of wealth, power, and authority, her loss and that of her community nevertheless break her. This type of grieving is an example of a spiritual principle reminiscent of the tiny-leaf principle in the story of Son of Raven. A broken person is like a humble person in the same way that becoming a tiny leaf humbled Son of Raven. Brokenness and humility become spiritual principles because it is discovered that beings of the spiritual realm respond positively when these principles are employed as communicative strategies. Sincere grieving from the heart is sometimes another acceptable way to access and influence the powers of the spiritual realm or to allow the powers of the spiritual realm to access and influence the physical realm. In either case, it can produce results. A being on earth initiates an action, and the spiritual realm responds according to its own purpose.

The response from the spiritual realm takes the form of a divine birth on earth. This is not a unilateral intervention by Qua-ootz, the Owner of Reality, but the result of a highly developed protocol that defines and guides communication and interaction between the two realms. Mucus discarded from the nose of the grieving *hakum* provides the means of accessing the spiritual realm from the physical realm. It is a mystery that makes no initial sense from an earthly perspective. Nevertheless, the divine birth of Aint-tin-mit (Son of Mucus) is a cooperative and interrelational act between "heaven and earth." Sincere grieving of the heart is consonant with spiritual activity in the spiritual realm. The heart of the *hakum* is broken and in pain. The discarded mucus is the physical manifestation of this brokenness and pain. The mucus, as a manifestation of brokenness and pain, comes alive naturally as a result of the inherent synchrony between heaven and earth. Its transformation into Aint-tin-mit is an interrelational act because of the intimacy created by the birth of a spiritual being into an earthly family and community. Thus, here again, *heshook-ish tsawalk* (everything is one).

Mucus does not have a good reputation in the public eye. Excess mucus from the noses of little children is a minor nuisance to them, while it may be considered dirty and unhealthy by adults. Excess mucus, as with an excess of anything else physical, may be a sign of disease, imbalance, or disharmony, as would inadequate amounts of mucus. However, mucus in a natural state serves a useful, mediating function. For example, on salmon, it serves to protect and preserve. If salmon slime is removed from its skin after it is caught, the salmon flesh will more readily decay.

In human nostrils, mucus serves the same purpose. If most of the mucus were to be removed from human nostrils, they would soon become irritated and easily subject to abrasions and sores. In perfect supply, the mucus in human noses allows both the free flow of natural air for life and an easy reception of smell. Mucus is a mediator of life. Aint-tin-mit (Son of Mucus) is a mediator of life. The lowly and despised mucus of the earth is a means for divine action reminiscent of the divine action achieved through a tiny leaf swallowed by the Chief's daughter in the story of Son of Raven. In this sense, *heshook-ish tsawalk* (everything is one); the Creator and the created, the Creator and creation, are intimately related in thought, word, and deed.

Boundaries and State Membership

Nevertheless, there are boundaries that must be observed. Aint-tin-mit had no legal rights to help the people until he was born into the community through the mucus of the Chief's wife. Spiritual beings are members of spiritual communities that have boundaries distinct from the boundaries of human communities. Membership in one does not automatically provide membership in the other. Rights in one community do not necessarily provide rights in the other. Aint-tin-mit achieved his rights through the Chief's wife and for the most noble of purposes: to save and rescue, to restore and make whole, to bring family and community together in a celebration of life.

In contradistinction to the birthright and legal membership status of Aint-tin-mit in the community of Ahous, Aulth-ma-quus has neither birthright nor legal membership. She is a thief, a killer, and, since her purpose in stealing children is eventually to eat them, a destroyer of life. She is the very antithesis of the design of creation. Aulth-ma-quus takes children that she has no legal right to take. She is an enemy of life and balance and harmony, an enemy of family and wholeness, and an enemy of interrelatedness. She is the inverse of a *quus* (human) living in community. Aulth-ma-quus has a home and a place to live that mimics the structure of family and community except that everything is reversed. She has a home, but it is not a home of harmonious relationships. The children in her home do not belong to her. Aulth-ma-quus's closest relationship is not to a human being but to an animated technology: a chamber pot. She is not kind, or friendly, or generous. Consequently, she has no friends, no community. She is alone despite all the children who live with her. The life of Aulth-ma-quus sounds very familiar to the modern ear: She is alienated, surrounded by people yet alone, and has a closer relationship with technology than with family.

Nevertheless, evil needs a home, a place to live. Traditional Nuu-chah-nulth spiritual practices and experiences indicate that good and evil are organized in the spiritual realm just as they are organized on earth. Thus, just as there are organized examples of goodness, organized charities, organized churches, we also have organized crime, organized gangs, and corporate corruption. In each organized group there is a leader. Aulth-ma-quus is a leader in her area. She is consistent. In this story she comes to steal children again, but by this time Aint-tin-mit has grown to become a young man. Fortunately, information about Aulth-ma-quus's whereabouts is available because of the child who managed to escape her clutches, and this is all the information that Aint-tin-mit requires.

What is the strategy that Aint-tin-mit employs to lure Aulth-ma-quus to her destruction? The strategy is "know your enemy." Vanity, or self-absorption to the exclusion of others, can be destructive to self and unity. Vanity to the point where the only person who matters is the one who is self-absorbed can be dangerous. Aint-tin-mit knew that Aulth-ma-quus was vain. There was nothing that she would not do for herself. Ultimately it resulted in her downfall because the original design of creation demands beneficial reciprocity. Individual beings are designed to help one another in order to fulfill the requirements of wholeness, balance and harmony, interconnection, and interrelationality. Therefore, to practise vanity as a lifestyle can be destructive.

The growth, development, beauty, fairness, and goodness of character of Aint-tin-mit can be perceived in different ways according to one's worldview. Where a dichotomy is perceived between the spiritual and physical realms, Aint-tin-mit provides a contrast between two worlds alien to each other. One is divine and the other earthly. One appears to be perfect, and the other appears to live along a spectrum that includes greatness and folly, good and evil, intelligence and stupidity, loving-ness and unkindness. However, when reality is perceived to be a unity, whereby one realm is the source for the other realm, Aint-tin-mit and Aulth-ma-quus are both suggestive of an original model of creation. Spiritual power marshalled against destructive power, as in the case of Aint-tin-mit against Aulth-ma-quus, is necessarily associated with Qua-ootz, the Owner of Reality, the Owner of Good and Evil. However, Aint-tin-mit is associated with the goodness of Qua-ootz, while Aulth-ma-quus is associated with *pish-shuk chiha* (bad spiritual power). That Qua-ootz is opposed to *pish-shuk chiha* is all that is indicated in this story.

It is significant that in the tension between the two spiritual models embodied by Aint-tin-mit and Aulth-ma-quus, it is not the destructive power that prevails but the creative power. The significance of the working out of this tension is that it adheres to a spiritual model reflective of the reality within the spiritual realm. This notion is a principle found within *heshook-ish tsawalk* (everything is one). In the spiritual realm there are opposing tensions, but the Creator remains the Creator, whose creative nature subsumes that which is destructive. Just as those associated with creative forces prevail over destructive forces in the spiritual realm, so too should those associated with the same kind of creative forces prevail over the same kind of destructive forces on earth. It is as though destructive, negative forces are necessary to *ha-mutt-sup* (show) the power of Qua-ootz.

The Means-Ends Issue

In her encounter with Aint-tin-mit, Aulth-ma-quus demonstrates her desire for the good things of life. After her disappointment that the beautiful image in the well does not belong to her, she immediately wants to know how she can become as beautiful as Aint-tin-mit. This is a common characteristic of thieves. They want the same things that the spiritually wealthy legitimately own. In this respect there is a commonality of goals between good and evil. The radical difference between the two ways of life is the means employed to achieve those goals. Aint-tin-mit is a model of integrity, honesty, generosity, courage, faithfulness, discipline, patience, goodness, and kindness, while Aulth-ma-quus represents the very antithesis of these characteristics. In this case, beauty is a spiritual principle that relies upon positive divine characteristics for its expression in the same way that ugliness relies upon negative characteristics for its expression. The choice of lifestyle can determine appearance. In this model, good characteristics such as generosity and kindness are associated with beauty, while bad characteristics such as thievery and destruction are associated with ugliness.

For the reasons noted above, Aulth-ma-quus had predetermined her tragic outcome from the time she began her thieving, destructive lifestyle. Her life and death are a fulfillment of her own choices. She lived by destroying children and consequently their families, and she died in the same way, with destruction of her self and her home. Why then would she trust Aint-tin-mit's alleged method of acquiring beauty? The reason may be that there is something authentic about the method suggested by Aint-tin-mit. The path to beauty, as with the path to greatness or success on earth, is apparently not through self-aggrandizement. Raven tries the "I am the greatest" path and finds that beings of the spiritual realm do not respond positively to this kind of approach. Only when he becomes a tiny, insignificant leaf, a harmless disposable, is he successful. In the same way, metaphorically, or in some spiritual sense, Aint-tin-mit did not acquire beauty on his own terms but on the terms of the Creator, Qua-ootz. It is possible that Aulth-ma-quus somehow vaguely recognized the divine origin of this principle of transformation. To become beautiful, a state that originates with the Creator, means to take on the characteristics of the source of beauty. The characteristics of a good person do not comprise selfishness, vanity, and egotism but generosity, humility, and a willingness to endure suffering and pain in order to access spiritual power. Aulth-ma-quus had only the former characteristics, not the latter, yet she seemed to recognize, without clarity, the relationship between pain and beauty. Consequently, she eventually conceded to Aint-tin-mit's suggestion that she be hit with a rock.

In traditional Nuu-chah-nulth culture, good and evil are not debatable questions. This is because, to the Nuu-chah-nulth, the world of good and evil is known and experienced collectively through the practice of *oosumich*. Consequently, in these communities the collective spiritual experiences of people determine human perceptions of the nature of the world. There can be no equivalent to a Plato, or a Socrates, or some such individual who might create a school of thought about reality that is later shared by some loyal followers. Rather, good and evil are determined by consensus through personal spiritual experiences that are reflected in the physical realm. Individual experiences are judged in the context of broad community experiences. For example, the individual practice of generosity has been found, over time, to be beneficial to personal, family, and community wellbeing, while the practice of theft has been found, over time, to be disruptive and destructive to personal, family, and community wellbeing. Individual experiences of generosity and theft and their outcomes have become generalized, communal experiences through public exposure.

These public exposures are commonly known as potlatches, feasts, or Nuu-chah-nulth cultural ceremonies. One of these ceremonies is known as the wolf ritual, or *tloo-qua-nah,* which might be said to be a re-enactment, in principle, of the story of Aint-tin-mit and Aulth-ma-quus. One perspective on the *tloo-qua-nah* ceremony regards it as an enactment of a loss of children to powerful outside forces (wolves in this case) and their subsequent rescue and restoration to the community. The principle of loss and restoration is common to both the *tloo-qua-nah* ceremony and the origin story about Aint-tin-mit and

Aulth-ma-quus. The literal translation of *tloo-qua-nah* is "remember-reality-we." The *tloo-qua-nah* ceremony is a community act of remembrance of the tensions between creative and destructive forces and the superiority of the former over the latter. It is a ceremony with a message of hope. It is good news for all who are oppressed, downtrodden, and beaten by the destructive dangers inherent to existence.

Good and evil are not amenable to empirical analysis because they are not empirical concepts; they are spiritual concepts. Good and evil can best be apprehended spiritually, not empirically. Consequently, a Nuu-chah-nulth canoe, as a concept and as an empirical fact, is an end product of human creativity, neither more nor less. In the hands of a good person, that same canoe can be used to promote a wholesome lifestyle. Using the canoe to capture seafood to feed a hungry family can do this. On the other hand, in the hands of an evil person, that same canoe can be used to kill and destroy other people.

Good may then be defined as those spiritual principles or values consistent with the character of creation, of Qua-ootz, Owner of Reality. Some of these principles or values survive today as *hahuupa* (teachings). In both a literal and metaphorical sense, these teachings have come down to people from Qua-ootz either directly through spiritual experiences or indirectly through the teachings of nature. For example, nature teaches that *heshook-ish tsawalk* (everything is one) through the now apparent interrelationship between each life form and the air, water, and land. On the surface of things it appears that created beings are so diverse that there can be no close relationship between them. However, as contemporary environmentalists and the scientific community have made clear, the entire ecosystem of the earth is a unity.

It is a small step from *heshook-ish tsawalk* to the teaching that the quality of relationships is very important. It is good to be constantly reminded of the Nuu-chah-nulth teaching always to be friendly toward others. This teaching is more than an encouragement to smile at strangers or to shake hands when introduced to someone today. It means that, in practice, if someone comes to visit in your home, you are encouraged to be hospitable. Usually, this will mean putting on the tea or coffee between mealtimes or serving a full meal at mealtimes. More specific, as mentioned previously, is the teaching about blood relatives. Always be very, very happy to see your blood relatives because your relationship to them is sacred and utterly valuable. Although this discussion appears to be a moral one, it can also be classified as a discussion about the nature of existence, about that which is an original design of creation. In this sense, to attribute value to kindness or friendliness is to describe how things were meant to be from the beginning, rather than some relativistic value that someone imagined.

Contextualized within these teachings is the value of generosity. The Western dictum that "it is better to give than to receive" is potentially misleading from a Nuu-chah-nulth perspective because an emphasis upon giving may lead one to consider receiving irrelevant or unimportant. In the traditional Nuu-chah-nulth view, both are of equal importance. Giving is completely dependent upon receiving, and receiving is completely dependent upon giving. There is balance and harmony here. Neither is generosity simply a romantic notion disconnected from the "bottom line" of harsh reality. Giving as a general community practice over millennia has proven pragmatic. It is an economically feasible principle.

The word potlatch comes from *pachitle* (to give). As always, there are appropriate and inappropriate ways to *pachitle*. Son of Raven gave an example of what the divine model is not. An inappropriate way to *pachitle* is the "I am the greatest" way, while the appropriate way to *pachitle* is through humility, as though, metaphorically, one were a tiny, insignificant leaf or despised mucus from the nose. This form of generosity, as a moral law, has proven to be true by community experience and consensus.

At the end of this first story of Aint-tin-mit, after he has rescued the children and brought them safely back to their homes, the community puts on a feast of thanksgiving. In addition to putting on a lavish and abundant display of food, the community would put on their best costumes, sing their best songs, and dance with all of their hearts, before also giving their best gifts to Aint-tin-mit. Although not mentioned, it would have been customary for Aint-tin-mit to receive a new name consonant with his exploits. This would be particularly true for the son of a chief's family. We can safely speculate that the new name would have been something in the order of Saviour of Children, Rescuer, Restorer of Families, or One Who Overcomes Evil with Good. It is a saga worthy of majestic and divine descriptions. The practice of great evil and the destructive powers that overwhelm those on earth have a heaven-earth remedy. The remedy points to a lifestyle that strives vigilantly to create and maintain strong loving relationships over a lifetime.

Son of Raven set the model for interaction with the spiritual realm. An inflated-ego approach to the spiritual realm is less acceptable than the humble approach. Neither the inflated nor the humble ego is testable or amenable to empirical analysis. These are discernible by and through the spirit. The story of Aint-tin-mit is the classical story of human beings who run afoul of evil. Aulth-ma-quus is an evil principle in the universe. Aulth-ma-quus is an evil spiritual reality in the spiritual realm in the same way that a mass murderer is considered an evil reality in the temporal realm.

Hope

Aint-tin-mit came to earth, to Ahous, to say to *quus* (humans) through his life and actions that creation naturally prevails over destruction. If people are overwhelmed in the face of a destructive power on earth, it likely means that they have forgotten the original model provided by Qua-ootz. The remedy is to remember reality, to *tloo-qua-nah*.

3 XAATS-STA

Thluch-ha ◈ Getting Married

This story about marriage takes place in the supernatural world. As an origin story it places the Nuu-chah-nulth custom of *thluch-ha* (getting married) into the authoritative category of having been created not by the Nuu-chah-nulth people but by Aint-tin-mit, a worthy representative of the spirit world. Significantly the path to a traditional Nuu-chah-nulth marriage is an adventure that reflects not only upon the individual act of union, but upon the very nature of being itself. The prospective groom is required to pass a series of difficult tests in order to qualify for marriage. Far from suggesting that marriage is like a walk in a rose garden, the tests indicate the challenges of the ever-present dangers inherent to existence. While marriage between two people is a truly carnal act, it is also a union of two beings, both of whom, like Aint-tin-mit, can have dual citizenship in heaven and earth. From a Nuu-chah-nulth perspective, this is the nature of being.

AINT-TIN-MIT RETURNS HOME

After a time Aint-tin-mit began to long for his original home. He told his uncle, "It is time for me to go home now." The uncle did not question. He simply accepted. Everyone grew sad at this news, but no one protested. Although Aint-tin-mit had been born on earth, they knew that he was also from some other place.

"I would like some arrows made. A great many arrows," Aint-tin-mit told his uncle. The uncle gathered the people together, and they were glad to help. Aint-tin-mit had saved their children and their future. They set to work,

Aint-tin-mit, Son of Mucus, shooting arrows into the sky. He used the arrows, made by a grateful Ahousaht people, to climb back up to his supernatural home. *Illustration by Cleesemeek*

splitting, cutting, shaving, and then carving the strips of wood into fine arrows. Day after day, week after week, the people fashioned arrows. No one had ever seen so many arrows at once. Each day the pile of arrows grew until Aint-tin-mit was satisfied.

Then one day Aint-tin-mit pointed to the sky and said, "Do you see there? There is the corner of my house, my home." The people looked and looked but saw only the sky. Then he took his bow and shot the first arrow into the corner of the house in the sky. Then he shot the second arrow into the first. The third arrow he shot into the second and on and on and on. The people watched the arrows disappear into the sky for a long time. And for a long time they could see nothing. Finally, when the arrows were almost all gone from the great pile, they could see a thin line of arrows disappearing into the heavens. When the last arrow was shot, the thin line of arrows was just high enough. Aint-tin-mit turned to his people and said, "I'm going back now to the place where I came from."

Aint-tin-mit began to climb. As he climbed he pulled out the arrows and dropped them to the ground. The people watched as he climbed. He seemed to grow smaller and smaller until finally he disappeared into the sky.

When Aint-tin-mit arrived home, he knew in his heart what he had to do, for he had returned to marry, and it would not be easy. First he must see the two old snail women. One was blind and the other almost blind. He went to their house and found them cooking. He decided to tease them good-naturedly. Very carefully and quietly, he took some food from the plate of one of the women. When she discovered the missing food, she turned to her friend and scolded her, "What are you doing?"

"Eh!" the other said in surprise.

"Why are you stealing my food?" the other replied indignantly. As the two old snail women quarrelled, Aint-tin-mit interrupted them with a chuckle. "Hold on there," he said. "Here's your food. I was only teasing. I'm sorry if I upset you."

"Ahh, is it you? We have been expecting you!" they chorused. "We knew that you would come back soon. The medicine to help you is ready. You know what you must do to win the Chief's daughter. At the entrance to the Chief's house, you will find a giant codfish. You must pass through this codfish to gain entrance. Next, as a visiting chief, you will have to sit near a great fire. You realize the loss of honour if you flinch before this fire. Finally, you must help the Chief split a great cedar log. If you survive these trials you will get what you want."

Then the old snail women gave him three bags of powder made from barnacles. This powder was a powerful medicine, and Aint-tin-mit thanked the old snail women for their help. He set off for the Chief's house. When he arrived he saw the gigantic codfish staring at him. Straightaway he entered the gaping mouth. Snap! The huge mouth closed and gigantic teeth gnashed together to grind him to pieces, to tear him to shreds and swallow him. But as the gigantic codfish's mouth closed on him, he transformed himself into mucus. The deadly teeth ground together harmlessly. Aint-tin-mit allowed himself to be swallowed, and so he emerged into the Chief's house, where he transformed himself back into a person.

The Chief came forward and welcomed him and asked him to sit by the fire. Even while Aint-tin-mit was being seated, the fire was being built into a roaring inferno. Hotter and hotter it grew. When the fire finally became unbearably hot, Aint-tin-mit took some of his medicine powder and threw it into the fire. Ho! The flames died down. Just as quickly the fire was built into a raging inferno again. Again, Aint-tin-mit reduced the inferno with some of his medicine powder. Time after time the fire was built up, and time after time Aint-tin-mit reduced the flames with his medicine powder. Finally, the fire remained small, and the Chief resumed the conversation.

"Way choooo! You wish to win my daughter!" the Chief said. "But before that happens I want you to help me to split a great cedar log." Aint-tin-mit agreed. The work began. Both the Chief and Aint-tin-mit worked expertly, pounding the wedges into the great log. It began to split. They pounded and pounded, moving their wedges from time to time. Carefully and slowly, the cedar gave way, making loud protesting noises. Then, while Aint-tin-mit was not looking, the Chief dropped a wedge into the great crevice of the split log.

"Go and get the wedge!" the Chief commanded Aint-tin-mit.

This was the moment Aint-tin-mit had been waiting for. He stepped down into the great crevice, and, as he did so, the Chief took out the rest of the wedges. With a crashing sound the enormous log closed on itself and onto Aint-tin-mit. At the same instant, Aint-tin-mit transformed himself into mucus and slid harmlessly out the end of the great cedar. This was now the fourth time that Aint-tin-mit's power had been tested (the first having been during his encounter with Aulth-ma-quus). Aint-tin-mit had been found worthy and so won the Chief's daughter.

The Nature of Being

Aint-tin-mit was both a *quus* (human) and a *chiha* (spirit being). He was both a son of the earth and a son of heaven. He had dual citizenship. He had rights in both worlds. Although Aint-tin-mit was from somewhere else, he was born into a Nuu-chah-nulth *hawilth's* (chief's) family. The Nuu-chah-nulth, rather than viewing this dual citizenship as extraordinary, as appears to be the modern custom, view it as a state of existence natural to creation. According to the origin story of Son of Raven, the duality of being is an original design. The two worlds, the spiritual and physical, were originally as interactive as any two closely related communities today. Travel, communication, and even intimacy between the two worlds were commonplace. One problem is that, over time, this original design can be difficult to remember as we become more and more fully engaged with such taxing earthly issues as maintaining the wellbeing of community, balancing individual with group rights, overcoming diseases, and simply hoping that survival is possible when difficulties appear insurmountable.

In fact, this is precisely the condition found in the community of Ahous that precipitated the deeply spiritual grieving of the *hakum* (chief's wife), resulting in the divine birth of Aint-tin-mit. The community of Ahous had evidently and gradually become less vigilant in its teachings and in its observances of these. The direct relationship between the loss of children to family and community and the relaxation of teachings and their observances is clearly and graphically illustrated in the *tloo-qua-nah* ceremony. In this ceremony it is common practice for the parents of the abducted children to be publicly chastised and accused of having forgotten the teachings of grandparents. Otherwise, their children could not have been abducted.

This forgetfulness renders the community more defenceless, and it consequently becomes vulnerable to the attacks of destructive outside forces, which in this case are represented by Aulth-ma-quus. When, in their duality, *quus* (humans) become more focused on their physical selves than on their spiritual selves, the imbalance creates a shortage of good spiritual power. The spiritual self weakens from disuse, from a lack of exercise. Physical power can be very potent, but it is insufficient for coping with all of life's challenges and problems. Aint-tin-mit's birth into the community of Ahous restored balance in the community and thus provided a natural means to overcome the destruction that imbalance may have created – an imbalance resulting from a laxness in teachings and observances and made manifest in the abductions enacted by Aulth-ma-quus.

Moreover, this circumstance of birth gave Aint-tin-mit the same rights of membership as other *quus*. If his community needed help, it was his responsibility, as *hawilth* (chief), to respond to that need. Aulth-ma-quus had threatened the destruction of family and community, and the forces of the spiritual and physical realms came together to overthrow that threat. Once Aulth-ma-quus is out of the way, Aint-tin-mit has other important things to do. He must return to the heavenly realm, the spirit world, but he cannot go by his own efforts, just as he could not have arrived without the help of the grieving *hakum*. There is a principle, or protocol, of reciprocity between the spiritual realm and earth.

The principle of free will and respect between the earth and the spirit realm must be maintained. Although the two realms are connected and interrelated, each realm has an independent identity. The spiritual realm does not ordinarily and arbitrarily exercise power over the physical realm. Just as Aint-tin-mit required the cooperation of the *hakum's* grieving in order to be born of the *hakum's* mucus, so too does Aint-tin-mit require the cooperation of the community in order to make an exit. Furthermore, it is necessary that the people have an opportunity to do something useful for the one who saved their children from destruction. It might be said that there is mutual recognition, mutual respect, and mutual responsibility between the spiritual and earthly communities. Qua-ootz, the Creator, Owner of Reality, does not exercise power arbitrarily over the lives of *quus* upon earth. There are protocols to be observed.

Pragmatically and quite naturally, Aint-tin-mit employed the familiar technology of the day to enlist the help of his community. Everyone knew how to make wooden arrows. It was a common skill that would provide an opportunity for everyone to put their teachings into practice. Consequently, when Aint-tin-mit asked people to help him, they were quick to respond. It should be remembered that asking for help is a very strong Nuu-chah-nulth teaching. *Wiikh-hay-itsk wik-qook huupee-is wa:* If you do not ask for help when you need it, you are not kind. As though it could not be emphasized enough, there was also a direct teaching to always *hupee-ee-aulth* (be helpful).

One can imagine that the community of Ahous, which held to such teachings, would not find it difficult to respond positively to the request for help from Aint-tin-mit. None would ever forget how Aint-tin-mit saved their children. Now they had a chance to do something in return to show their thanksgiving to, and their love for, their saviour. So they made arrows. These arrows, it turned out, would be used to show the natural connection between the two realms: that of the earth and that of the spirit. The people made the arrows with their own hands, and these same arrows made by *quus* hands performed a (super) *natural* act. Aint-tin-mit caused these arrows to fly straight up to his own house in the heavens. All the arrows flew straight and true, into each other, end to end, until a solid line of arrows was made between the house in the spirit world and Aint-tin-mit standing on Nuu-chah-nulth soil. Every member of that Nuu-chah-nulth community who helped to make the arrows was represented in this connection between heaven and earth, between *quus* and Qua-ootz, the Creator.

The connection between heaven and earth illustrated by the arrows makes manifest that which is ordinarily invisible. No *quus* on earth can see Aint-tin-mit's house, but eventually they do see their own arrows as these come closer to the earth through the connectedness of each arrow to another. If this connection is to be made, each arrow must be straight and true, not crooked and false. Is this not a teaching, a *hahuupa? Apstii-yook up-in* (make our paths straight; help our lives to go in the right direction) are the usual words of petition in daily Nuu-chah-nulth prayers. Each arrow represents a *quus* on earth whose life must hit the mark, whose life must be straight and true. Each arrow is fashioned and created by each *quus*, by each person. Every decision made about how the arrow is created, from the time it is a formless piece of wood until it is a finished product ready to fly upward, is made by the *quus*.

Even the decision to make an arrow that is intended to fly upward is a major undertaking. It requires a great deal of planning, commitment, endurance, patience, faith, and hope. Unexpected problems and disappointments lurk at every turn. It is very easy to give up, to throw in the towel, to put on a jaded air of skepticism, to believe in your own inability, rather than in the ability of the spiritual and earthly realms to work together through sincere prayers and effective communicative strategies. This is the reason for the Nuu-chah-nulth teaching that two voices come from the spirit world: One voice comes over the left shoulder to entice one to evil, while the other voice comes over the right shoulder to encourage one to do well. In this worldview, each person is guided through life at every turn.

The arrows made for Aint-tin-mit were destined to fly straight upward. Some arrows are made to fly elsewhere. They may be badly made, or made from poor grade wood, or made with shabby tools, and these will surely miss the mark. They can be made to destroy rather than to create, to fly toward death rather than toward life. However, everyone who helps Aint-tin-mit to return to his original home in the spirit world is shown the way. Aint-tin-mit becomes a role model. All those who wish to fly upward can do so by following the role model. Aint-tin-mit has a purpose in life that is fulfilled. It is a good purpose. He comes to save lives, to help *quus* in distress. This is how to make a life into a good, straight arrow: by fulfilling a good purpose. The pattern of life demonstrated by Aint-tin-mit is that of a life in family and community. Such a life is respectful of all life forms and dedicated to the wellbeing of others; it is an enemy of evil forces that seek to disrupt and destroy the integrity of family and community.

Thus, as Aint-tin-mit begins to climb back home, he drops each arrow back to the earth. The arrows are of the earth and so return to the earth once their purpose has been fulfilled. It is the same with *quus* bodies; they go back to the earth when their time on earth is fulfilled. Once Aint-tin-mit arrives back in the spirit realm, his first act is to good-naturedly tease the two old snail women who have been expecting him. Apparently, serious business and funny business are two sides of a well-balanced coin. In the midst of great endeavours and exploits, there is also a time for fun, games, and laughter.

Having fun provides relief from one serious activity and a healthy transition to another. Later, the old snail women will recall this event with merriment and fondness: merriment at themselves and fondness for their beloved Aint-tin-mit. There is a word for this kind of fun. It is called *wee-kee-chitl*. This phrase can be translated as "a time to divest of all responsibility." Literally, the phrase means "to be in a state or condition of not doing, of not performing that which was being performed." Consequently, at great formal feasts demanding extended periods of solemn ritual and observance of protocols, there comes a time for *wee-kee-chitl*. It is a time of fun and merrymaking that is as relaxing as the formalities are taxing. It is transformative. It is cathartic. It is healthy and very deliberate. The songs and dances for this fun time are called *kwee-qua-thla*. Although the *kwee-qua-thla* is meant to be highly entertaining, it is always performed in a ceremonial context that honours the host chief. The degree of skill displayed in the *kwee-qua-thla* is the measure of pride displayed toward the host. Teasing the old snail women, as a form of *wee-kee-chitl*, is a perfect way for Aint-tin-mit to re-enter the spirit realm because later, on his way toward marriage, he will face severe trials of faith and courage.

Aint-tin-mit's marriage signifies a divine principle of relationships, which, in the earthly model, translates into one individual marrying another. The divine principle is the unity of creation, *heshook-ish tsawalk* (everything is one). *Heshook-ish tsawalk* is the divine principle of marriage. When two marry, according to the earthly model, they become *tsawalk*, one. In this sense, marriage is a formal expression of the general characteristic of creation, which is relationality. Creation is designed so that each being is fulfilled through relationship with another.

Aint-tin-mit's difficult route to marriage signals the constant tension between good and evil in creation, the inherent tension between creative and destructive forces, between positive influences and negative influences. Aint-tin-mit's journey toward marriage began when he grew up and decided to rescue the children that Aulth-ma-quus had stolen. This was his first test. After returning to his home in the sky, his next test was to gain entrance to the Chief's house through the mouth of the giant codfish. In succession, he then had to withstand the heat of a great fire and to escape entrapment within the giant crevice of a great cedar. Although the unity of creation, the principle of oneness, is a basic assumption to the earthly model of marriage, the principle of the unity of creation cannot be taken for granted because contrary forces may seek to destroy this unity. In this sense, marriage for the Nuu-chah-nulth has a divine, rather than a human, orientation.

Aint-tin-mit's great struggle against evil in the person of Aulth-ma-quus, against fear in the form of a giant codfish's mouth, and against natural destructive forces in the form of a great fire and a giant cedar log represents a struggle with the destructive forces that may test the worthiness of a man for marriage to an *usma:* the precious, the beloved, the revered. It was unthinkable to regard marriage as a spur of the moment decision. Marriage required a lifetime of preparation. Aint-tin-mit had been preparing for a lifetime. He was a model son of a chief. He learned all of his lessons, the *hahuupa* (teachings) of his house. He chose to live in, and work for, the Nuu-chah-nulth community. He was respectful and humble. He was strong and brave. He became a son of the earth, but he was also a son of heaven. He never complained about the order of creation. He lived the original design.

Aint-tin-mit's great struggle toward marriage mirrors the anticipated struggle to remain married. Marriage can be beautiful, wonderful, satisfying, and even euphoric, but it can also be characterized by struggle. A marriage requires constant work because reality is characterized by a constant tension between good and evil forces. Any relaxation in the forces of unity means an advantage for the forces of destruction. When a state of harmony in marriage is achieved, it is through creative work characteristic of Qua-ootz.

The father of the intended bride is not surprised by Aint-tin-mit's visit. This is because he has been informed, likely at the time of his daughter's birth, of Aint-tin-mit's intention. This practice is known as "childhood betrothal" in English. Irrespective of the father's long-held knowledge, it is necessary to test the apparent commitment to marriage. The testing and trials endured by Aint-tin-mit before his marriage became mirrored in marriage practices of the Nuu-chah-nulth. For example, during the 1940s, a chief's family from the Mowachaht tribe of the west coast of Vancouver Island travelled down to Ahousaht and camped around our house for four days. They had come for the hand of my aunt Nora, whose marriage had been arranged between the two families when she was still very young. The arrangements were made during one of the many intertribal ceremonial feasts at which different families came together and took the opportunity to discuss many important matters. At the appropriate time, when Nora had turned sixteen and the suitor family had completed all the planning and preparation conducted over the years, the ceremonies began. As the Mowachaht approached Ahousaht territory, the house of Keesta was alerted. It would by no means be a surprise visit. The house of Ahinchat, Keesta's son, expected this visit in the same way that Aint-tin-mit's visit is anticipated by the father of his intended bride.

Although the arrangements are made many years before, an intended marriage does not automatically take place. It is a betrothal, a promise to marry on the proviso that certain conditions are met. Some conditions must be met prior to the visit. The intended groom must have demonstrated his ability to support a bride and family. The suitor family must have everything in readiness for a wedding feast. Then, during the visit, the suitor family must give voice to the rationale for the marriage.

It is an exercise in mutual recognition, continuity, and consent between two extended families. Each extended family recognizes the status position of the other as equal. Each family is a chief's family. It is a marriage between two extended families that are equal, and the consummation benefits both communities. The better the quality of a chief's family, the greater the benefits for the community, for this is how chiefs' families are defined: by the quality and quantity of benefit that accrues to community. This social, economic, and political arrangement ensures continuity for the community, and it is brought about by mutual consent. It is mutual recognition, continuity, and consent between two extended families for the benefit of the larger community at the apparent expense of individual choice.

My aunt Nora had no personal choice in the matter. She did not personally know her intended groom, Edward Anthony Jack, except by sight. She knew that her cousin Sheila was Edward's girlfriend. However, an indication of the weak influence of Western ways during this time is that Edward and Sheila's relationship created not the slightest stir after the marriage was consummated. No gossip made the rounds; no rumours about Edward's girlfriend created any schism in the strong fabric of Nuu-chah-nulth life ways that had been strengthened over millennia by ceremony and respectful protocol. In the middle of the twentieth century, when many social scientists bemoaned the disappearance of Aboriginality, important ceremonial aspects of Nuu-chah-nulth life ways continued unabated in the same manner as they had for centuries previous.

Gilbert Sproat was one of a few who provided first-hand accounts of Nuu-chah-nulth life as it must have been lived prior to contact. He wrote in 1860 of the Nuu-chah-nulth that he had not heard oratory as great as theirs, not even in England. It should be noted that oratory that moves human beings must have some extraordinary qualities, including a systematic order of thought, balance and harmony between ideas, sound projection, inflection of voice, fluency, and a facility with words that is both creative and responsive to the minds and hearts of its listeners. Yet the oratory typical of the precontact Nuu-chah-nulth described by Sproat was not unusual. Among the Nuu-chah-nulth, people from every tribe were trained from birth to become orators and speakers for great, chiefly personages.

Trudy Atleo (left) and Nora Jack outside their father's house at Ahousaht, mid-1940s.

Outside Ahinchat's house, one of these orators, so trained from birth, would have lifted his voice and announced the presence of one of the descendants of the same Maquinna who had greeted Captain Cook 167 years earlier in Friendly Cove off Nootka Sound. The oration outside Ahinchat's house would have begun by identifying the groom's father and with an account of some of the greatness of his lineage. There would have been an account of his *hahuulthi* (ancestral territory) describing its vastness and the resources that belonged to the chief of the family. There would have been an account of other social and political assets, but all these accounts did not by themselves ensure that a marriage would take place. It might have been that all this great oratory was just a bunch of wind without real substance, much like the oratorical wind commonly coming from today's politicians. The oratory, as impressive as it was, had to be accompanied by a pragmatic demonstration of some kind of *tupati* (spiritual power). A *tupati* is an inheritance acquired through a *chih-shitl* encounter, or spiritual experience, that can be used for the benefit of the extended family.

To demonstrate his *tupati,* for example, a member of the groom's family might be required to hit a sealskin target with a bow and arrow from a distance, say, of forty feet. The arrows, however, will not be weighted with any kind of arrowhead. Of course, it is the weight of the arrow-

Florence (Flossie) Atleo (left) and her older sister Nora Jack (née Atleo) at a more contemporary wedding feast in Thunderbird Hall at Ahousaht, early 1970s. Nora's own wedding took place after the ancient customs of the Nuu-chah-nulth.

head that provides stability and allows for accuracy. Without the weight of the arrowhead, the target becomes much more difficult to hit. A related example of such a demonstration might be a family member's ability to hit the sealskin target from, say, ten to twelve feet away with a large eagle feather. The feather is naturally curved and ordinarily unstable in flight; moreover, to increase the degree of difficulty, the feather must be thrown tip first rather than shaft first. What is the point? It is believed, because it has been observed many times, that people who have acquired spiritual power through *oosumich* should be able to fulfill the requirement of a *tupati* demonstration. When the groom's family exhibits this kind of spiritual power by hitting the mark, they are allowed into the big house to begin the final phases of a Nuu-chah-nulth wedding.

In the meantime the visitors, as happened to Edward's family, will find that their seagoing transportation has been let loose and set adrift. Normal social protocols are held in abeyance during these times. No one moves to help the visitors with their problems because it is necessary to see if they are serious about this union between two families. When Edward's family discovered that their transportation was gone, they had to retrieve it by hiring local people. In addition to such unexpected expenses, there was also the cost of travel, the cost of the ceremonial

Meeting inside Chief Keitlah's house, at Ahousaht, c. 1914 (between 6 and 23 May). This big house was designed to hold several contemporary-sized nuclear families, as indicated by *sta-kumlth*. *RCBM NO 12513*

feasts, and the bride price (given to the groom's family), which ensure that only chiefs can engage in these kinds of activities. When everything is satisfactory to both families, all the preliminary testing ceases, and the celebration of wholeness begins. Gifts such as names, songs, and economic rights to land or resources may be exchanged to strengthen alliances, which is consonant with the intended purpose of wholeness in creation.

Nuu-chah-nulth people did not form nuclear households as they do today but became members of a big house, of a *sta-kumlth* (extended family). Ordinarily, upon marriage, a woman joined the big house to which her marriage partner belonged. She took on the identity of another house while maintaining relational ties to her biological family. This is what happened to Nora. She was brought to Yuquot, where she was ceremonially heralded as a new *hakum* (chief's wife) of the Mowachaht. In pre-contact times this ceremony would have been conducted from two large canoes lashed together with a platform as they slowly approached the landing site of a beachfront. In Nora's time the ceremony was conducted from the bow of a contemporary fishing vessel.

Extraordinarily, my great-grandfather Keesta had the right to *cha-koop-ha*. This chiefly right meant that Keesta could bring the groom into his house to live instead of sending his granddaughter into another house. Therefore, when his granddaughter (my aunt Trudy) married, she brought her husband into Keesta's house. She did not go into the house from which her husband had come. Instead, they became a part of Keesta's *sta-kumlth,* a part of Keesta's house and lineage. In a real sense, a Nuu-chah-nulth marriage was less between two people and more between two lineages, two extended families. Marriage, therefore, was about the constant creation and maintenance of family and community branches, of *sta-kumlth,* each of which could be traced to common roots.

Balancing Individual and Group Rights

Nuu-chah-nulth marriage customs appear to be tyrannical by modern standards. There is no question that postmodernity is prevailingly individualistic while optimistically espousing plurality. Despite postmodernity's rejection of modernity's one worldview, there persists at all levels of modern society imbalances between individual and group rights. Because the prevailing focus upon individualism runs counter to the ideals of plurality and equality, there has been, it seems to me, an intensification of alienation and fragmentation within society.

If the high divorce rate is any indication, one could conclude that some (or even many) married couples in North America do not strive for family rights but for individual spousal rights. And apparently every individual's rights have been violated in some way or other, which in turn demands redress by law. A strict accounting is kept of every spousal act – the number of extramarital flings, the times the dishes were done, meals made, children dealt with, mail picked up, phone calls made, personal clothes bought – and inevitably deficits accumulate. Neglect or over-indulgence by one spouse in one or more areas of accounting soon becomes intolerable. Although there must be some marriages that constitute sound, loving relationships, there are other cases in which marriage is not a game of love and friendship, of give and take, of live and let live, but a game of rights, a game that requires a strict vigilance so that one partner is not short-changed in individual rights guaranteed by the Constitution of Canada. This state of affairs in postmodernity might justifiably be described as a tyranny of individual rights to the exclusion of, or to the detriment of, group rights. There appears to be an imbalance between the two.

By comparison Nuu-chah-nulth marriages appeared to balance the two kinds of rights. First, the big house structurally facilitated the existence of and focus upon the group in Nuu-chah-nulth society. Each big house had room for several nuclear families. A chief who governed the house could not make decisions unilaterally because of a prevailing worldview that demanded consensus in decision-making processes. Thus there was a balance between individual and group rights. In this world-view, each person was to be respected because of his or her association with Qua-ootz, Owner of Reality, Creator of All. This respect was extended to all life forms for the same reason. A translation of this respect into the practice of living is that each life form, each individual person, must be allowed to be whatever Qua-ootz intended. The contemporary phrase "to walk in your brother's moccasins" means more than to empathize with your brother's subjective experience; it refers to cultural practices that allow an individual maximum freedom in making his or her own choices in life, in determining his or her own road through life, providing these choices do not violate group rights.

These egalitarian cultural practices, whereby each life is respected as a unique expression, extended to the marriage relationship. In the context of Nuu-chah-nulth culture and its values, men and women in marriage were free to pursue their own interests. These interests, in traditional Nuu-chah-nulth life, might have ranged from developing the skill to manage a household to developing food- and medicine-foraging skills, developing artistic or musical skills, and developing shamanic powers that would have rivalled the powers of the greatest chief in the community. Women who developed shamanic or medicinal powers usually did so under the mentorship of an *ushdaxyu* (elder shaman). *Ushdaxyu* literally means "one who has completed spiritual training and acquired power." This power could be manifested in prayer chants, songs, and dances or through the application of specific medicinal herbs.

There are examples of women developing their individualism in the recent oral history of the Ahousaht. According to one story told by my grandmother Margaret, there was a Cowichan girl, a daughter of a chief, who did not want to marry the man to whom she had been betrothed since birth. She ran away and was found by Ditidaht hunters, who brought her to their chief. As was the custom in administering the chief's *hahuulthi* (ancestral territory), she became his slave; according to the precepts of territorial sovereignty and ownership of resources, the chief took possession of anything or any person found within the *hahuulthi* boundaries. The Ditidaht chief threw a great feast and *pachitled* – that is, gave his newly acquired slave girl to a chief from Ahous. The Ahousaht chief brought the girl home, where she proved herself by performing all the customary purification rituals and prayers alongside her master. She was not obligated to perform these difficult rituals, but neither was she forbidden. The decision was entirely personal, an individual right, even for a slave. She was the only slave girl to do so since it was usual for most, if not all, slaves to forgo the pain and discomfort. After a time, it became apparent to the Ahousaht chief, both from the girl's willingness to endure the rituals of nobility and from her regal bearing, her self-discipline, and her quick intelligence, that she was much more than a slave in spirit. Ultimately the Ahousaht chief gave a great feast and raised this slave girl from her lowly position to sit by his side as a *hakum* (queen).

My aunt Trudy's husband, Edwin, tells another story demonstrating a woman's freedom to pursue her own talents. He relates how a woman, during the time of his father, had the power to take the spirit out of a person and put it back again. Since, by this time, European settlement had begun in Ahousaht territory, some *quus* (people) had already become infected with the newcomer's skepticism about the supernatural. Consequently, the woman asked that a dead squirrel be brought to her. Then she asked for a volunteer, and a man by the name of Ollie stepped forward. She told him not to be afraid and that he would not remember anything about the demonstration of her power. She performed her ritual, and Ollie fell down as though unconscious. She picked up the dead squirrel and performed her ritual, and suddenly the squirrel began to run around the room. After a while she asked that they capture and bring the squirrel to her because it was dangerous for Ollie to be separated from his spirit for any length of time. She performed her ritual on the squirrel again and upon the unconscious Ollie, and both reverted to their original states: the squirrel lay dead on the floor, and Ollie regained consciousness. He did not remember a thing.

What is true about the freedom of women in marriage is equally true about the freedom afforded men. Within the context of family and community, they too are free to pursue their own interests in the same way. Individualism in Nuu-chah-nulth society, then, is practised to the utmost for the wellbeing of family and community. That is, individual interest and individual self-expression of the kind pursued by the slave girl are intended to serve the interests of family and community. Shamanic and medicinal powers are developed in the interest of family and community life.

The harsh rituals demanded of a chief are likewise performed in the interest of the wellbeing of family and community. Keesta enacted his rituals in order to capture a whale and thereby attain food and oil for the wellbeing of his community. The slave girl became a *hakum* because she met the standards set for a *hakum*. My grandmother Margaret reports that when she bathed with her husband, Chief Ahinchat, her long black hair froze into icicles as she emerged from the bathing pool. She was not required to accompany her husband, and neither was she forbidden. Her sacrificial expression of individualism was well balanced with her interest in the wellbeing of her community group. She found a satisfactory personal expression in serving the needs of family and community. Thus *isaak* (respect) for all life forms manifested itself in the relationship between Ahinchat and Margaret, both in his respect for her individualism and in her respect for the community served by the bathing ritual.

What Is Freedom?

When an extended family makes a decision about marriage with another extended family, it appears to be a violation of individual rights. It is said that, in prearranged marriages, the freedom of choice is taken away from the individual. This is certainly true in a social environment that is focused upon the rights of individuals. However, the price for this kind of freedom appears to be very heavy. There is a significant difference in terms of physical and monetary resources, social support, availability of experience, and human power between the marriage of two individuals and the marriage of two extended families. An extended family offers more physical resources, more money, the support of more people, more experience as embodied in the grandparents, and greater security from outside threats than does a nuclear family developed by two individuals.

The irony of a society that prizes individual rights above all else is the apparent tyranny that develops from the very practice of individualism. Married couples that focus on their individual rights to the detriment of the welfare of the marriage suffer the tyranny of individualism. The practice of individualism can be so strong as to become the enemy of the family because the nature of existence defines each person as unique: no two individuals can be found to be identical; each is different from every other. When two people marry and their focus is on individual rights, their uniqueness will condemn their marriage to the negative consequences of their imbalanced view of life. In contradistinction, when two extended families form a union, there is greater latitude for individual uniqueness since the make-up of an extended family is more diverse than that of a nuclear family. When problems of marriage arise in the context of an extended family, the experience of older members can offer solutions that have proven practical. Support is built into extended family groupings.

4 M U U

Quis-hai-cheelth ⬡ One Who Transforms

As a chief's name, Quis-hai-cheelth may refer to the power that a person has for transformation. The name is a clear reference to the events that take place in the origin story of Raven. Raven and his community easily and effortlessly transform themselves into sockeye salmon and salmon-berry shoots without losing their original personalities. Whether as a salmon, salmonberry shoot, or tiny leaf, Raven remains essentially Raven. Transformation and change are major themes of the Nuu-chah-nulth reality and worldview.

Aint-tin-mit and Biodiversity

In the Nuu-chah-nulth's precontact experience, life is full of problems, but it has a hero who not only becomes their rescuer but also provides the means for the transformations that bring about the biological diversity evident today. Since all life forms have a common origin, all the earth's diverse beings are to be treated according to the demands of this common origin. According to the Nuu-chah-nulth, this origin is divine: this origin is Qua-ootz, Owner of Reality. The sacredness of a common origin determines the basis of relationships between diverse life forms.

Aint-tin-mit had one more task that would change the appearance, if not the commonality, of the life forms of the world. In those days there were no animals as we know them today. There were only people. Without contradiction, these people were Raven, Deer, Wren, Woodpecker, Wolf, Eagle, Grizzly Bear, Salmon, Skate, Dog Fish, Loon, Crane, and so on. In those days, too, there were people who could foretell the future. The prophetic word had been given that someone was coming to change people into something else. Everyone wondered about this prophecy. The great chiefs (Wren, Eagle, Woodpecker, and Grizzly Bear) held council. After much thought and discussion, they decided that they did not want to be changed into something else. Moreover, they decided to kill anyone that tried to change them. The people began to make ready and to fashion weapons.

Upon Aint-tin-mit's return to the earth, he found Raccoon carving a beautiful club with many designs. With a friendly smile Aint-tin-mit approached. He had been gone for so long that he was now a perfect stranger. He saw that Raccoon was almost finished.

"Haaww! You have a beauty there!" Aint-tin-mit said.
"Raccoon! What are you making?"
"It's a club!" Raccoon said proudly.

Aint-tin-mit as Transformer, when he created biodiversity. *Illustration by Cleesemeek*

"Ooh!"

"Haa-uh [Yes], it's for the one who is coming to change people into something else."

"Ooooh!"

"Haa, but if he tries anything with me, wham, I'll get him with my club."

"Here, let me see it." Aint-tin-mit said admiringly. "Haaww! It is beautiful! Very beautiful! Here, turn around, Raccoon. I think it would look nice right here." Then Aint-tin-mit placed the club on Raccoon's backside, slapped him there, and said, "Go. Henceforth, you shall be Raccoon!" Away scampered Raccoon as an animal.

As Aint-tin-mit walked on, he soon came upon Deer making two knives from seashells.

"What are you doing?" Aint-tin-mit smiled.

"Oh! I'm making knives," Deer said.

"Haaww! That is fine workmanship!" Aint-tin-mit declared.

"Haa-uh!" Deer paused to admire his own handiwork. "I'm preparing for the one who is coming to change people into something else. I like me exactly the way I am! No one is going to change me!"

"Haaww! Let me see those!" Aint-tin-mit said. Deer was flattered by the stranger's interest and handed the knives over. "Hmm, these would look very pretty on your head." Aint-tin-mit smiled. "Haa-uh, that will do!" And with that Aint-tin-mit slapped Deer on the backside and declared, "Go! Henceforth, you shall be Deer." And away Deer bounded into the forest.

And that is how Aint-tin-mit made every manner of animal and life form that inhabits the earth today. Each weapon he admired flattered each person to whom it belonged. To each he said, "Go. Henceforth you shall be ..."

Thus today we have wolves, deer, bears, raccoons, ravens, eagles, and all the rest of creation.

A Common Ancestry

In the Nuu-chah-nulth worldview every life form is of one *thli-muhk-sti* (spirit), of one essence. Contrary to the classical Western view, the Nuu-chah-nulth do not assume that humans have one type of life essence or spirit and the bear another. Both, in the beginning, were of the same essence, of the same *thli-muhk-sti*. Observed differences between the human form and other life forms are products of transformations that resulted in the adoption of different types of outward "clothing" by each. The raven has a feather coat, the bear has a fur coat, the salmon has a fish skin, and people have human skins of different colours. When they all take off their clothing, it will be found that each is like the other in spirit, in essence. This is one of the fundamental assumptions of traditional Nuu-chah-nulth cultures because it is inconceivable that the Great Spirit would not reify itself in creation. The source of creation is found in the Creator, who established the life principle of *like producing like*. When the principle of free will is introduced, it becomes possible for life forms to have both an Aint-tin-mit and an Aulth-ma-quus effect, both a creative and a destructive effect. Once decisions are made for good or evil, seeds produce after their own kind: an apple seed produces an apple tree, and a pear seed produces a pear tree. Evil does not issue from a good heart, and neither does good issue from an evil heart: *like produces like*. This is a spiritual concept, a spiritual principle, rather than a biological imperative. Biological diversity is the result of an intelligent, transformative act performed by Aint-tin-mit. Of course when changes are made to creation's design, it is the Creator who issues the orders and creatures such as Aint-tin-mit who carry out the orders.

Protocols between Life Forms

The worldview wherein all life forms, human and nonhuman, have a common origin as completed creations of the Creator has implications for the life ways of a people. One of these implications is the development of laws to govern relationships. In *The Spirit in the Land* (1992), Gisday Wa and Delgam Uukw, two hereditary chiefs of, respectively, the Gitksan and Wet'suwet'en nations in British Columbia, explain that the relationship between all life forms, human and nonhuman, is the foundation for their law. "The land, the plants, the animals and the people all have spirit – they all must be shown respect. That is the basis of our law" (Gisday Wa and Delgam Uukw 1992, 7).

Later they go on to explain the rationale for this law:

The Western world-view sees the essential and primary interactions as being those between human beings. To the Gitksan and Wet'suwet'en, human beings are part of an interacting continuum that includes animals and spirits. Animals and fish are viewed as members of societies that have intelligence and power, and can influence the course of events in terms of their relationships with human beings ... The Gitksan and Wet'suwet'en believe that both humans and animals, when they die, have the potential to be reincarnated. But only if the spirit is treated with the appropriate respect. If bones of animals and fish are not treated with that respect, thereby preventing their reincarnation, then they will not return to give themselves up to humans. (Ibid., 23)

Constitutional, federal, state, provincial, and municipal laws are oriented around human issues and concerns, while Gitksan and Wet'suwet'en laws are oriented around humans, animals, and spirits in an equitable, or balanced, relationship. Gitksan and Wet'suwet'en laws are typical of indigenous worldviews. These laws are meant to maximize the wellbeing of life forms, human and nonhuman.

Representation is key to the development of all laws. For example, the salmon people, through spiritual means of communication such as a vision quest, will inform humans of the specific protocols necessary to maintain balance and harmony in the salmon-human relationship. In a very realistic sense the salmon are meaningfully represented at the treaty negotiations between the salmon people and, say, the Gitksan and Wet'suwet'en people or the Nuu-chah-nulth people.

Violations of these laws have natural consequences since they create imbalances that undermine the equitable character of completed creation as it is experienced and shared by all life forms, human and nonhuman. Clear-cut logging practices, strip mining, over fishing, and immoderate hunting practices are all examples of disregard and disrespect for nonhuman life forms. Whether the current environmental crisis being experienced by the earth is explained by an indigenous worldview or by science, the conclusion is the same: the environmental crisis is a crisis of imbalance and disharmony between human and nonhuman.

Transformation or Change as a Natural Condition of Creation

It appears that one of the major themes of creation is transformation or change. Things and life forms do not just hold still. Existence appears to be dynamic rather than fixed. In the story of Son of Raven, a major change is created by the introduction of light into the world. Light enabled people to see more clearly as they continued to learn how everything in creation works. They already knew where they had come from because they assumed an intimate relationship to their source of creation, the Great Hawilth (Chief), Qua-ootz, Owner of Reality.

They shared a common language and assumed a common heritage because they were all *quus* (human) and thus related. They felt entitled to the benefits available from the spiritual realm, the source of all creation. They learned that nothing was gained without their effort, careful planning, cooperation, initiative, vision, hard work, patience, endurance, persistence, faith, and hope. They learned also that nothing is gained from the spiritual realm without observing an appropriate protocol, without discovering effective communicative strategies, which demand humility. After some time their lives reflected the intent of the original design of creation for that time, for that phase of creation. They fulfilled this design by building upon the lessons learned during their interactions with the spiritual realm. They were well oriented to creation's design and consequently became set in their ways. They began to feel that the familiar pattern of their lives should go on forever. It was time for a change, for a transformation. The design of creation had completed an important phase. One of the signs of the need for such change may be the development of a resistance to change.

Contemporary Transformations

According to one interpretation of the Nuu-chah-nulth view of history, there is a pattern to existence that relates to the development or fulfillment of purpose. The birth and life of a modern human today demonstrates, in general, this pattern of existence. First, there is the infant phase, during which, from the baby's perspective, reality is such that self and the immediate source of life – the mother and the nourishment of her breasts – remain undifferentiated. The baby grows and grows and develops many skills. All things being equal, by age five it has mastered and fulfilled every requirement for life during that phase. There could be a parallel in meaning between the phrase "set in their ways" and completion of a phase of life. In September, when it comes time to enter kindergarten, it is not unusual for the five-year-old to resist the change. The child, it can be said, has become "set in his or her way." The child is now familiar with every aspect of a pattern of life at home. From the time the five-year-old awakens in the morning until it is time for bed at night, he or she is completely at home with everything in the house. There is usually nothing left to discover or investigate. The social growth of that child, in that home environment, is now at an end. Further social growth will require an extension to this limited home environment. Kindergarten is that extension.

Resistance to change in the kindergarten scenario may be called *phase resistance,* a "phase" here being one complete stage of existence that is connected, and related, to an indefinite number of other complete stages of existence. Consequently, in the life of a child, the first phase takes place in the womb. When that phase is completed, the birth takes place. During the birth process it is usual for the mother to experience birth pangs. These birth pangs indicate phase resistance. The resistance takes place at the juncture of two connected and related phases: life in the womb as a foetus and life outside the womb as a newborn baby. The next major phase resistance takes place at the juncture between life in the home as a baby/toddler and life at school as a kindergarten student. Each phase is subdivided into minor stages of development or change. The newborn baby changes from a completely helpless person – unable to feed itself, unable to move, unable to speak – into a progessively more independent person. Leaving behind immobility, the baby soon develops the ability to turn over, then to crawl, then to stand, then to toddle and totter, and eventually to walk. This same pattern to existence can also be recognized in the global movements that have been identified as modernity and postmodernity.

Modernity to Postmodernity

The colonial enterprise – and its one undifferentiated people, language, nation, and hegemonic form of modern constitutionalism (Tully 1995) – is now giving way to a more differentiated, multicultural, pluralistic expression that has come to be known as "postmodern." The colonial enterprise, at least in the Western world, seems to have completed its natural phase of existence, socially, politically, economically, and spiritually. The presumed supremacy of Western colonizers, in all these areas of human activity, is now called into question. The missionary-inspired rationale for colonial dominance over the earth and its indigenous inhabitants, the spread of so-called superior European civilization, can now be *ha-mutt-shitl* (revealed/unveiled) for its substantial shortcomings as a world order.

With the brilliance of hindsight, it now appears infantile to consider the extant resources of the earth unlimited. Colonial descriptions of the "new world" were filled with such notions as: buffalo as far as the eye could see; untold numbers of birds that darkened the sky; salmon so thick on the rivers that one could walk on them. Yes, the earth's resources were without limit when considered in the context of a smaller world population and a more primitive technology. In this colonial context, it made some sense to develop the economic goal of maximum exploitation for maximum profit. The "new world" was perceived as a source of unlimited wealth by an "old world" that had exhausted most of its own resources.

Suddenly, toward the end of the second millennium, the inhabitants of the earth, who have been brought together through the technological developments of modernity, awaken and become outraged at the devastation to their planet, their only home. The land and its environments, the oceans, seas, and the air, are all polluted to such an extent that if paradigmatic changes are not begun immediately, the extinction of at least the human species becomes possible. Not only is the earth, as a place of habitation, unhealthy for humans, it might now be argued that this modern civilization has been unable to achieve its goal of good government. War is a constant, while order seems as fleeting as a night's sleep. In short, the goal, set by colonials, of civilizing the world has failed. The colonial experiment by the Western world appears to be over. The earth is now suffering from the anguish of the birth pangs that must usher in the full force of postmodernity. If a postmodern perspective is not achieved, humans may not survive much longer, the pattern of life designed by modernity being so inherently destructive. The earth's biosphere has been severely damaged and is in need of emergency repair.

Phase Resistance as Natural
The economic practice of maximum exploitation combined with technological development meant that modernity, as a completed stage of existence, would coincide with an environmental crisis. It appears quite self-evident that you cannot have change without friction. It is natural, then, in the face of impending paradigmatic changes to the world order, that there should be friction. Clayoquot Sound, on the west coast of Vancouver Island, became a focus of environmental protest over the clear-cutting of rainforests. The international attention drawn to Clayoquot Sound forced the BC government into action that resulted in the formation of a scientific panel in 1993. In 1995 the provincial government accepted the panel's recommendations for changes to forestry practices in Clayoquot Sound that were designed to protect the health of the forests.

Phase Transition
These recommendations highlighted phase transition from modernity to postmodernity because they signalled a move away from clear-cut logging to resource extraction that considered the health of forests to be equal in importance to profit. Logging in Clayoquot Sound must now be done in such a way that the forest is left in a state of health that

allows not only the trees, but also the life forms that depend on the trees, to survive.

Nevertheless, there is resistance to change. At a recent conference on the environment at the University of British Columbia, one of the presidents of a forestry company remarked that citizens do not want to lose the benefits of clear-cut logging. Yet change is inevitable. The Government of British Columbia changed its forest-practices code so that these practices could, over time, become ecologically friendly and sustainable. It appears that the majority of the youth segment in society have already made the adjustment. By the time these youths mature, and take the reins of power and influence in society, the transition to post-modernity may be in full force.

Toward the end of the twentieth century, paradigmatic changes had already begun for the Aboriginals of Canada. Through the lense of modernity, the Aboriginals were considered primitive and childlike. This attitude is reflected in the Indian Act. Aboriginal people and communities as self-governing entities with jurisdiction over their own sovereign territories were not recognized. The 1997 Supreme Court decision in *Delgamuukw v. British Columbia*, which made oral histories permissible under Canadian law for the first time, is helping to change that. Aboriginal title to land, previously held in question, can now be recognized because of the *Delgamuukw* case. The hegemonic, one-world-order perspective of Canadian law has given way to the plurality of post-modernity by recognizing another perspective on land title.

If change, and resistance to it, is a natural condition of existence, the experience of change and resistance must be universal to life forms. The treaty-making process in which the Nuu-chah-nulth are currently engaged is an example. Every Nuu-chah-nulth alive today has been born into a world governed by the precepts of the Indian Act. There have now been five generations of Nuu-chah-nulth so born. The Indian Act has created a culture of its own with which the Nuu-chah-nulth are now completely familiar. They understand how the health care system works. They understand, for the most part, where they can and cannot shop with tax exemption. They understand what it means to be a status Indian, with a status identity card, on reserve and off reserve. They are now set in their ways. The protection provided by the state through the Indian Act has now become customary to their way of life, an assumption of Nuu-chah-nulth existence. In this social context it might be expected that, despite constant complaints against the tyranny of the Indian Act, there would be resistance to any change. There is.

In December 2000, at the conclusion to preliminary treaty discussions with Canada and BC, those at the Nuu-chah-nulth treaty table initialled an Agreement in Principle (AIP). Several of the Nuu-chah-nulth communities rejected this AIP, which meant that the entire Nuu-chah-nulth treaty table had to do the same. The Nuu-chah-nulth protocol in dealings with one another is that all must be in favour or there can be no agreement. Not unexpectedly, there is great fear among Nuu-chah-nulth members about the possible terms of any treaty. The fear is primarily about loss. The focus of discussions in my own community of Ahousaht was about loss. We will lose land, we will lose marine resources, we stand to lose future resources, and so on. This has been the talk from the majority. There has been little talk of an affirmative kind, little talk about challenges, about opportunities. It is easy to see why resistance to change is a natural condition of existence. Who knows whether the forthcoming changes will not be disastrous compared to the familiar comforts of the present?

Phase Connector

While "phase resistance" describes an unwillingness to accept change, and "phase transition" describes the process of change, "phase connector" describes the substance or medium that effects the change. Examples of phase connectors can be found in origin stories. Examples of substances used as mediums of change in these stories are the club that turns into Raccoon's tail and the shell knives that turn into Deer's ears. Whenever the Nuu-chah-nulth see raccoon or deer today, they can be reminded of the first age when all life forms were undifferentiated in appearance, before the age of biodiversity. The club and knives are representative of a mature phase of existence and thus indicate that the design of creation has been fulfilled for that time. For this reason, the phase connectors are always the materials or skills acquired during a particular phase.

Figure 2 models some of the characteristics of phase resistance, phase transition, and phase connectors. Phase transition takes place naturally through the fulfillment of the purpose of a phase, and the means of transition are the outcomes of the phase itself. In the phase transition that is taking place between modernity and postmodernity, scientific knowledge about devastation to the earth's environment has become an important phase connector. Earth's environmental crisis signals the maturation of a phase.

Figure 2

Phase transition

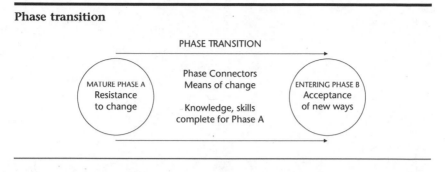

Among humans the Aboriginals of Canada have also been experiencing a variety of crises: of educational failure, suicide, substance abuse, violence, sudden-infant-death syndrome, poverty, family and community dysfunction, and a number of health issues such as AIDS, diabetes, and asthma. The colonial agenda to recreate the Aboriginal of Canada after the image of the European has been a colossal failure in all dimensions of human existence, the social, political, economic, and spiritual. During this time of failure, the Aboriginal has acquired the language and many of the skills necessary to cope in an environment of dependency created by the colonial enterprise through the Indian Act. These acquirements are phase connectors to another life that may be more like the independent way of life familiar to their precontact ancestors.

Remember Common Ancestry

The story of Aint-tin-mit and biodiversity reminds Nuu-chah-nulth people about the natural relationship between all life forms. How can the story of Aint-tin-mit do this? First, Aint-tin-mit is both a *chiha* and a *quus*, a spirit being and a human being. This duality of being is a reminder of the nature of existence at the beginning of time, when travel between the two realms, earth and heaven, was common. Raven and his people could transform into plants or animals at will as easily as people change clothes today. Second, biodiversity, a purely physical phenomenon, is brought about by transformations effected by a *chiha*, a spirit being, Aint-tin-mit. *Heshook-ish tsawalk;* everything is still one. The models of transformation are still there as though waiting to be remembered again.

5 SUH-TCHA

Thlawk-thlawk-qwa A Humble Petition

Thlawk-thlawk-qua (a humble petition) is the approach discovered by Raven in his quest to bring light into the Nuu-chah-nulth world. It is a major key that unlocks the door and makes the resources of heaven available to the earth. The "tiny, insignificant leaf" approach to *oosumich* is the great spiritual secret of the ancient Nuu-chah-nulth – which, when successfully practised, opened the spiritual storehouse of power, medicinal information, knowledge, and wisdom. Although there were three principal sources of knowledge for precontact Nuu-chah-nulth (origin stories, *oosumich*, and nature), this chapter will focus on the spiritual component common to each source of knowledge. My treatment of this spiritual component is divided into sections discussing the *oosumich* method, the necessity of spiritual protocols, and the necessity of ritual cleansing in order to acquire knowledge. My great-grandfather Keesta is used as a prime example to illustrate this practice of Nuu-chah-nulth knowledge acquisition.

Nuu-chah-nulth Knowledge Acquisition

As indicated in earlier chapters, origin stories provide an orientation to the design and meaning of creation that is then tested by the *oosumich* method, which is guided by certain protocols. Essentially this design reveals that everything and every life form are of common origin. This is consistent with the big-bang theory of modern science, which postulates that the known universe came into existence from a singular explosion. Science is unable to explain how the explosion came to be but recognizes that the current activity of the universe is indicative of a big bang. However, Nuu-chah-nulth origin stories teach that there is a natural relationship between creation and the source of creation. There is a natural relationship between that which was made and the Maker. There is a natural relationship between the spiritual and the physical. What remains is to discover how that relationship works effectively. Nuu-chah-nulth origin stories indicate clearly what is effective and what is not effective in that relationship. This section focuses primarily upon the *oosumich*, or spiritual, approach to Nuu-chah-nulth knowledge acquisition.

Supernatural Experiences and Survival
"Have you had a fearful experience?" my aunt would ask me in our language when I was a little boy. "Fearful" is a rough English translation of the Nuu-chah-nulth word *chih-shitl*, which refers to a supernatural experience between a human and the spirit world. In my family, the Atleos, as with all Nuu-chah-nulth families, supernatural experiences were necessary for an effective management of reality. This chapter provides a few examples of the countless untold stories of supernatural experiences among the Nuu-chah-nulth. Although no argument or apology will serve to sway a pure empiricist, it is well to say that these experiences are neither isolated to a few who may not be quite right in the head nor the outcome of widespread mass hysteria or delusion. The reason for this claim is that all these significant experiences are testable. This means, for example, that a *chih-shiltl* experience that results in the acquisition of healing power is testable among the public through a systematic demonstration of healing.

There are many stories that indicate a positive test of healing powers acquired through *chih-shitl*. In general all such experiences may be classified according to one of two orientations: The first is the spiritual orientation, wherein the experience is initiated from the spiritual realm; and the second is the human orientation, wherein the experience is initiated from the physical realm through the usual means of fasting, meditating, ritual cleansing, praying, petitioning, waiting, and chanting. Each of these orientations or methods is discussed in the context of the examples given later in this chapter.

I was eighteen months old when I had my first *chih-shitl* experience. It is my family's story that my father spoke to me after he drowned. He said, "Everything will be all right." In Nuu-chah-nulth life, this type of *chih-shitl* experience is very common across a wide spectrum of people spanning the precontact, modern, and postmodern eras.

Other experiences may be initiated in the spiritual realm during the ordinary course of human activities. A person may be berry picking and suddenly witness a most unusual event, such as a tiny ball flying through the air in a self-controlled fashion, as though it were being controlled by an intelligence, or as though it were an intelligence itself. These are fearful experiences that often require appropriate responses in order to be completed. My own response to the experience with my father, who had just drowned, was to tell my family about it, and they remember it to this day. How much trust does an eighteen-month-old have toward his father? There was no room for philosophy or rational doubt in this communication between the temporal and spiritual realms. My father spoke, and it appears that his word has come true: I am now writing this book more than sixty years later. In terms of my survival and a small measure of success in life, my father's word has come to pass.

When these types of experiences happen to an older person, as in the case of one who is berry picking, there are established protocols to be observed. These protocols have been passed down from generation to generation. For example, if confronted by a tiny ball flying through the air in a self-controlled way, custom would dictate a specific response. Since, for practical purposes, this kind of information is usually kept secret, it is necessary to create here a make-believe response. Let's say that the appropriate response to this "fearful" event is to retrieve the little ball and bury it in a forest. This type of response determines whether the proposed transaction between the spiritual realm and the physical realm will be completed. If completed there will be a transfer of some gift, some power, from the spiritual realm to the physical realm. The participant in the "fearful" event would acquire some right to some gift or power. This right, this gift, might be medicinal or some other power. If the recipient is ignorant of the protocol and does not respond appropriately, the transaction cannot be completed. At most, the recipient will now have a story to tell. Inevitably the storyteller will become the recipient of unsolicited information from relatives with pertinent experience about the appropriate protocols to observe should the event ever occur again.

The hypothetical case of the berry-picking experience is one of the more mundane types, of which there are a great many possibilities. "Fearful" experiences can take an infinite variety of forms, but all involve a communication process between the spiritual and the physical. That which is communicated between the two realms, the spiritual and the physical, is critical to the physical realm. The crux of this chapter is about the manner in which knowledge is acquired from the spiritual realm when the communication process is initiated from the physical realm. This process is commonly known in the English language as a "vision quest."

A Fearsome Environment

The term "vision quest" has been used in English for convenience of communication. One interpretation of the Nuu-chah-nulth word *oosumich* would be "careful seeking" in the context of a "fearsome environment." The environment is fearsome in two dimensions of reality: the physical, given the dangers inherent to a mountain wilderness; and the spiritual, whose inherent dangers have been long known. Eugene Arima defines *oosumich* as a "purificatory bathing ritual featuring fasting, continence, staying in cold water, scrubbing the body with bundles of twigs and other substances, and praying to the Sky Spirit[1] or Moon" (Arima 1983, 10). The first syllable, "oo," means "be careful." It is used in different ways in different contexts. In a spiritual context it invokes supernatural fear – that is, human fear in the presence of spiritual mystery.

In everyday life the "oo" is used in the same way that concerned parents the world over utter the words "be careful" when sending their children out to play. Even in this everyday usage there is an inherent assumption that life can be dangerous. On the west coast of British Columbia, when children learn, at a very young age, how to swim in the ocean, they are often cautioned: "Don't swim out too far! Stay close to the shore!" Similarly when the young go out fishing or hunting by themselves for the first time, they are always sent off with parental warnings about the weather and other possible dangers. The fabric of life is interwoven with a variety of good and bad, a variety of blessings and curses. Life presents itself as a challenge. In order to meet this challenge successfully, the Nuu-chah-nulth understood the necessity of accessing significant power from the spiritual realm.

Humans have natural power and ability, but it is very limited in comparison to the great powers available from the spiritual realm. For this reason, the vision quest is considered vital to survival and to the effective management of reality. As mentioned earlier, it is not the concern of this book to discuss the variety of visions that humans experience, whether in a nocturnal dream, waking dream, meditative vision, group vision, or solitary vision, but to focus upon the spiritual experience itself that results in the acquisition of knowledge and power that can be demonstrated. One of countless numbers of Nuu-chah-nulth who practised this methodology of knowledge and power acquisition over millennia was Keesta.

My Great-Grandfather Keesta and Authenticity

Since the first line of criticism about anything indigenous is to seriously question the authenticity of any claim to Aboriginality, it is necessary

Keesta with baby Eugene Peter Atleo, a first cousin of the
author, in Ahousaht, c. 1948.

to explain the context of Keesta's early personal life in order to determine whether the degree of Western influence during these early years
could be deemed significant.

Many of us from Ahousaht can trace our lineage back to the same
ancestor. Those with the modern Ahousaht surnames of George, Benson
(Keitlah), and Atleo, along with their extended families, can trace their
ancestry back to Cle-shin, who lived around the mid to late 1500s, about
400 years ago.[2] In the fourth generation descended from Cle-shin, the
Georges and Bensons (Keitlahs) split off into two chieftainship lines
that began with Chiefs Hashiyacmis and Tawinism respectively. In the
fifth generation descended from Cle-shin, the chieftainship of the Atleo

line appears, beginning with Chief Ah-up-wha-eek, who is a younger son of Tawinism. During the ninth generation descended from Cle-shin, Keesta's father, Chief Nokmis, appears in the 1891 Dominion Census of Canada, together with Keesta, who is listed as Atlu. Chief Nokmis's age is recorded as fifty-five years, and Keesta's age is recorded as twenty-five years. That would place their dates of birth at 1836 and 1866 respectively. However, certain younger contemporaries remember Keesta as being older than the recorded census indicates. Relative to younger contemporaries and relative to his father, it is highly likely that Keesta was closer to thirty years old at the time of the 1891 census.

During this period of Keesta's life the fur trade had been in existence for about one hundred years. Wilson Duff, in *The Indian History of British Columbia,* remarks about this period that "the fur trade produced no major revolution in coast Indian life, compared, for example, to the effects of the horse and the gun on Plains Indian life. But it brought prosperity, an increase in wealth in a society already organized around wealth ... The new wealth strengthened the existing social and economic systems rather than weakening them" (Duff 1965, 57).

Robin Fisher, in *Contact and Conflict,* concurs that the fur trade on the Northwest Coast enhanced, rather than minimized, indigenous cultures: "Clearly the fur trade brought change to Indian society, and yet it was change that the Indians directed and therefore their culture remained intact. New wealth was injected into Indian culture but not in a way that was socially disruptive, so the cultures were altered but not destroyed ... The impact of the fur-trading frontier on their culture was creative rather than destructive" (Fisher 1977, 47-8).

Although new material goods were brought into the homes of indigenous peoples along the Northwest Coast, these goods did not alter in any significant way their values and general way of life. They continued to eat their own foods, live in their own homes, speak in their own ancient languages, and perform their ancient rituals and ceremonies, which were now enhanced by the influx of new material goods, such as blankets and iron tools.

Change is not unusual to any culture or civilization, yet it is assumed that as soon as change is introduced to indigenous cultures, they can no longer be considered authentic. Authentic indigenous cultures are thought to be those that have had no contact with the colonizing Westerner. It is a most arrogant position to hold because it attributes inordinate and unreasonable powers of transformation to the colonizers. Rolf Knight is one author who appears to hold this unrealistic assumption.

In *Indians At Work: An Informal History of Native Indian Labour in British Columbia, 1858-1930,* he writes: "In sum then, by 1858, at the beginning of massive European settlement, no truly indigenous and unchanged Indian society remained in BC. They had all undergone variable but considerable degrees of change. They were neo traditional Indian societies undergoing further change. Much of what is today popularly held to be the original, the pre-contact cultures of Indian peoples were partly the formations of the eighty year fur trade history. There were both continuities with past indigenous cultures and newly emergent forms" (Knight 1978, 233).

In a historical and social sense the issue is one of *voice.* In a political sense the issue is one of self-determination and self-governance. A good example is the early anthropological description and designation of the west coast of Vancouver Island's inhabitants as "Nootkan." These same people have since replaced the word "Nootkan" with "Nuu-chah-nulth," and this name is recognized at the treaty table. The Nuu-chah-nulth have reclaimed or asserted their own *voice* and are now negotiating self-governance with both Canada and British Columbia. Neither the issue of *voice* nor that of self-governance was of concern to Keesta and his contemporaries during the late nineteenth century; although the Indian Act had been instated in 1876, its effects could not be immediately felt in the more remote communities, such as that of the Ahousaht. Prior to 1876 Keesta's father, Nokmis, exercised the ancient sovereignty of *hawiih* (chiefs, kings) over territorial waters and land. A century earlier, in 1792, the Spanish explorer José Mariano Moziño described, in a first-hand account of the Nuu-chah-nulth people, an organized society with a system of governance: "The government of these people can strictly be called patriarchal, because the chief of the nation carries out the duties of father of the families, of king, and high priest at the same time. These three offices are so closely intertwined that they mutually sustain each other, and all together support the sovereign authority of the *taises*" (Moziño 1970, 24).

The *taises* (also spelled *tyee, tais,* and *tighee*) refers to the eldest male offspring, who holds hereditary rights to a seat of governance and attendant territories, together with their resources. This highly organized society, described in some detail by Moziño, was typical of the Nuu-chah-nulth of the time. This first-hand observation and other accounts in a similar vein by Captain Cook and others are in marked contrast to the unfounded speculations of early European armchair observers such as Thomas Hobbes, John Locke, and Jean-Jacques Rousseau. It is apparent that these early European speculations continue to be an influence since the Honourable Chief Justice Allan McEachern partially quotes Hobbes when he describes precontact Aboriginal life as "nasty, brutish, and short." Hobbes's more complete but speculative description of Aboriginal life reads: "No arts; no letters; no society; and which is worst of all, continual fear and danger of violent death; and the life of man, solitary, poor, nasty, brutish, and short" (Hobbes 1651, 96).

Locke and Rousseau, during the seventeenth and eighteenth centuries respectively, agreed with Hobbes, imagining that Aboriginal peoples did not live in organized societies but roamed the forests, each person alone, in a wild and instinctive manner. Rousseau imagined (what would Freud have said about such a wild fantasy?) an Aboriginal male copulating with a female that he had met incidentally, like two strangers passing in the night forest never to see each other again, the male never to know his own offspring.

Chief Justice Allan McEachern, apparently persuaded by these speculations and many others since,[3] wrote in his judgment in *Delgamuukw et al. v. The Queen:* "In their opening, counsel for the plaintiffs asserted that the plaintiffs have formed a distinctive form of confederation between their Houses and clans and that they have always enjoyed a level of civilization which is at least equal to many others which have received much greater prominence. The defendants, on the other hand, point to the absence of any written history, wheeled vehicles, or beasts of burden, and suggest the Gitksan and Wet'suwet'en civilizations, if they qualify for that description, fall within a much lower, even primitive order" (McEachern 1991, 31).

After casting doubt upon the claims of the counsel for the plaintiffs, McEachern goes on to conclude that: "I have no doubt life in the territory was extremely difficult, and many of the badges of civilization, as we of European culture understand that term, were indeed absent" (ibid.). The unfounded speculations of Hobbes, Locke, and Rousseau about the state of life of Aboriginals become articles of faith because these writers are long-deceased; thus the study of their ideas in every law and political science class has contributed to the widespread negative stereotyping of indigenous peoples.

However, what is apparent to the contemporary Nuu-chah-nulth was not apparent to Keesta. During his early years he grew up in the manner familiar to his ancestors prior to the arrival of any European colonizer. Although Eugene Arima (1983) notes that mission stations had been established as early as 1875 (Roman Catholic at Hesquiat), 1893

(Methodist at Nitinat), and 1896 (Presbyterian at Ahousaht), the Nuu-chah-nulth life ways of thousands of years remained intact well into the twentieth century. Despite the encroaching legislation of the Indian Act and the activities of agents for the Ministry of Indian Affairs in concert with the police, all of which were intended to undermine Nuu-chah-nulth sovereignty and plenary authority, ancient ceremonies still took place on a regular basis, particularly during the nineteenth century. Even during the first quarter of the twentieth century, these ceremonies, which reflected Nuu-chah-nulth sovereignty, continued to occur, albeit secretly.

Robert Thomas of Ahousaht, born in 1920, and my father, Eugene Atleo, were childhood friends, and Robert often recounts how during his early years his mother, Fannie (née Keitlah), would take him to secret ceremonies at Klaqkishpeethl, the house of Keesta. Since all "potlatching" had been outlawed, they would always have guards or lookouts posted in case any government authorities happened along. At a feast in Port Alberni in November 2000, Robert Thomas related an incident that took place in Ahousaht during the first half of the twentieth century. A residential school had been set up a little distance from the reserve, and the school staff had gotten wind of a *tloo-qua-nah* ceremony taking place at Klaqkishpeethl, the house of Keesta. The residential school staff attempted to gain entry but were foiled by sturdy doors and guards. The residential school staff were suspicious but could not obtain any direct evidence. According to the Indian Act, the *tloo-qua-nah* ceremony was a criminal activity, but the *tloo-qua-nah* that took place at Klaqkishpeethl during that period was not an isolated incident among the Nuu-chah-nulth.

In his book *Potlatch* George Clutesi, a Nuu-chah-nulth author of the Tse-sha-aht nation provides a first-hand account of a *tloo-qua-nah* ceremony that took place during the 1920s. It is now commonly held that the early missionaries understood all indigenous ceremonies to be the work of the Devil. Anthropologists such as Philip Drucker and Eugene Arima understand the *tloo-qua-nah* to be a wolf ritual because of the prominence that wolves play in the ceremony. However, in my view, the *tloo-qua-nah* may be a wolf ritual in the same way that the holy sacrament of a Christian church may be viewed as a bread ritual. Christian churches have a ceremony in which bread is eaten in remembrance of the body of Christ, the Son of God. To call this Christian ceremony a bread ritual might lead one to misunderstand the sacrament as a trivial ceremony rather than one involving remembrance of the Son of God.

The *tloo-qua-nah* ceremony involves wolves, but it is principally a ceremony to remember the Creator. As stated previously, the word *tloo-qua-nah* may be broken up into its three syllables. *Tloo* means "to remember"; *qua* means "reality," or "state of existence"; and *nah* means "we." Therefore, *tloo-qua-nah* can mean "we remember reality." However, one of the Nuu-chah-nulth words for God, as stated by Chief Maquinna at the time of first contact and recorded by Moziño, is "Qua-ootz." *Qua* means "reality" and *ootz* means "owner of." The word "Qua-ootz" is not an actual name of God, or the Creator, but an indirect reference to the Creator. This manner of indirect referencing is typical of Nuu-chah-nulth culture because of the importance and power of names. It is reminiscent of Jewish culture, wherein God's name is considered too holy for human utterance. *Tloo-qua-nah* is much more than a wolf ritual. It is a ceremony in remembrance of the Owner of Reality. Clutesi echoes the observations of explorers such as Captain Cook and Moziño when he notes that "along the entire coast of Vancouver Island established areas were acknowledged to belong to tribes, with Kings who exercised plenary authority over that area" (Clutesi 1969, 31). The fragment cited below of a formal and customary speech given at a *tloo-qua-nah* ceremony clearly embeds the *tloo-qua-nah* inextricably within a display of sovereign activity by a Nuu-chah-nulth nation:

THE SPEAKER

Choo why, choo why. Hear ye, hear ye.
Rulers, chieftains, queens, revered young ones,
Braves, clansmen, commonalities, all.
Listen you now, for the voice of this house,
Whose seats you have graced with your person.
It will utter, yea, with many voices will it utter ...

Hear again the stories that are old;
Traditions that our ancestors told.
The laws they made are still with us.
They are here and have not changed.
Our Lands, our streams, our seas remain
To provide for our wants, that are yours and mine. (Ibid., 35)

The above speech was one of many that took place during the first quarter of the twentieth century. *Hahuulthi,* or the traditional territories, mountains, lakes, streams, rivers, and foreshore and offshore fishing grounds owned by *hawiih* (chiefs), together with its attendant laws, was well understood among the several Nuu-chah-nulth communities. The concept of *hahuulthi* was not unknown to the first trickle of European settlers, some of whom obeyed its tenets by returning objects to rightful Nuu-chah-nulth owners. Rights to items of value found in a *hahuulthi* area were always, according to Nuu-chah-nulth law, taken to the owner of that *hahuulthi*, who would then pay or reward the finder. The pace of life at that time allowed the *tloo-qua-nah* ceremony to be fulfilled during a complete cycle of the moon, twenty-eight days. In the latter quarter of the twentieth century the *tloo-qua-nah* has been revived, as it is no longer outlawed, but its performance has been vastly reduced from a ceremony lasting several weeks to one that might take one weekend to complete.

It can now be said with some certainty that Western influence had little impact upon the main core of Keesta's early life. Although a mission school was established in Ahousaht in 1896, Keesta may already have been well into his 30s. His early schooling and training were highly specialized, befitting an heir to a chieftainship, and entirely after the manner of his ancestors. From his mother's womb, according to ancient custom, he heard the songs and teachings about his ancestors, his identity, and his future promise as a chief. Through story and song, he heard and understood the meaning of his people, the meaning of his land, and the connection between spiritual power and the acquisition of resources for the wellbeing of his people. Inevitably he would have been exposed, at an early age, to the sights and sounds of every important ceremonial gathering of Klaqkishpeethl, the house of Keesta. At an age considered preschool today, he would have begun to train by diving into the ocean every morning during certain months of the year. This training is called *tupsweese,* and its practice survived into my generation. As a little boy, before breakfast every morning, I would *tupsweese.* I was taught to *tupsweese* by my grandfather, Ahinchat, who was taught by Keesta, who was taught by Nokmis, who was taught by his father, and so on back into time immemorial.

The significance of Keesta's early training in life as an example of precontact Nuu-chah-nulth ways cannot be overemphasized. Clearly the influence of the settlers who arrived after he became a man was negligible. The fur traders, who arrived before Keesta's birth, brought new materials into Keesta's culture, but these new materials served to enhance rather than to alter the heart and soul of a way of life. Consequently Keesta's life can now be presented as a lived example of one who, in the traditional manner of his ancestors, practised the "vision quest" with visible results.

Keesta was born among the Ahousaht, who are now principally located on Flores Island on a reserve known as Maqtusiis.[4] Flores Island is located between the now world-famous Long Beach, just south of Tofino, and Friendly Cove to the north, where Captain Cook and others met Chief Maquinna to establish a fur trade.

Because Keesta survived into the early 1950s, it was possible for my aunt Trudy, the youngest sister of my father, with her husband, Edwin Frank, to live with Keesta after her marriage. This arrangement was no accident; as explained earlier, Keesta was a *hawilth* (chief) who had the right to *cha-koop-ha*. That is, in the marriage of his granddaughter, my aunt, he could bring the groom into his extended family. Consequently, my aunt's husband became a member of Keesta's extended family and was given the name Kwascha-a, which he earned as a result of an *oosumich* during a rising tide. Although Edwin received the name as a very young man, this name was not publicly revealed until March 2001. During a memorial feast convened by George Frank, Umeek (direct descendant of Keesta) *ha-mutt-sup* (made public) the name Kwascha-a. This story is significant because it illustrates two points. First, concealing a name until it can be appropriately made public is a precontact practice. It is a

View of Ahousaht from Russell Channel, c. 1914. The house in the centre of the village belongs to Chief Keitlah and the one to the right of it belongs to Keesta. *RBCM PN2398*

Trudy and Edwin Frank in their home at Ahousaht,
6 August 1976. They lived with Keesta during the first
decade of their marriage.

prime example of an ancient practice that has survived into the present
century. Colonial interference prevented the appropriate disclosure of
the name until 2001, some fifty years later.

Second, Edwin has testified in family conversations that this name,
and the power it represents, is responsible for any success he has enjoyed
in life. Not only has Edwin faced and overcome significant challenges
in his life, but his successes have endured for over half a century. This
endurance factor is a strong point in the name Kwascha-a. It is a very
powerful name befitting a chief's family because the name refers to a
bathing ritual during the winter that extends continuously from low
tide to high tide, an agonizing six hours of *oosumich*. Edwin had to earn
his name before Keesta could grant it to him. It was Keesta himself who
instructed Edwin. Outsiders who have since had to conduct business
with Edwin and have found themselves being bested, overcome,
outlasted, and somehow convinced that Edwin's proposed solution must
prevail probably had no idea that they were up against Kwascha-a. And
they never will know unless they happen to read this account.

What follows now will not be an actual account of specific practices of
the vision quest because these are family secrets. They are not only family secrets but also "oo," spiritually fearful secrets, which lose their power
and effectiveness when revealed to others. The principle of spiritual

secrets, or mysteries, is a common idea but not part of the subject of this book. Rather, what will be presented are the broad outlines of a way of life, together with specific references that illustrate a practice without disempowering it.

The Spiritual Methodology of Knowledge Acquisition

The Atleo family's *oosumich* time (careful seeking in a fearsome environment) was from November to February. However, the actual ritual preparation time might have taken eight months for a major expedition, such as a whale hunt. Of course, it was not a whale "hunt" in the same sense as a commercial whale hunt, where all the planning, preparation, and execution take place exclusively within the physical realm without any communication with the spiritual realm. It was more of a secret agreement made between life forms, such as that made between Keesta and the spirit of the whale, that represented a fulfillment of the design of creation. Figure 3 presents a simple model that purposely separates the spiritual and physical realms in order to illustrate the *oosumich* methodology.

The *oosumich* model serves to show that the source of success in the physical realm is found in the spiritual realm. This Nuu-chah-nulth spiritual methodology serves as a research instrument for testing the validity of origin stories. For example, the story about Raven bringing the light to the physical world demonstrates that there is an orientation to the nature of creation that can be made to work to the benefit of people on earth. Raven paved the way for the *oosumich* methodology through his own series of tests. He found the egotistical approach ineffective and the humble approach effective.

Figure 3

Model of *oosumich* methodology

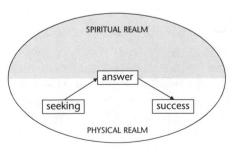

Consequently, if light is said to originate in the spiritual realm, the *oosumich* method should verify this teaching. If the wolf, bear, deer, and salmon are really people who simply have outward clothing distinct from that of *quus* (people who wear skin), the *oosumich* method should verify this teaching. The positive consequences of adhering to good teachings, such as the instruction to be kind, friendly, and generous, have been endlessly verified within Nuu-chah-nulth culture, as have the negative consequences of breaking with such teachings. Metaphorically, good teachings are of the light, while false teachings embody dark and destructive power. Since the beginning of all things, when the story of Son of Raven was first told, these teachings have been translated into practice and their truths affirmed by common Nuu-chah-nulth experience.

There were traditional whalers who were successful and traditional whalers who were not successful. This is a critical point because the Nuu-chah-nulth had a way of life whose objectives were fulfilled according to the characteristic range of human abilities. In the contemporary world, where both stereotyping and romanticizing are common practices, it may come as a surprise to read an Aboriginal account that presents a balanced view of human conduct. The stories of Raven clearly teach that human behaviour may range from the ludicrously stupid to the gloriously wise, intelligent, and brave. The characteristic range of human abilities suggested by these origin stories is still evident in every society and institution today. Superior, average, and poor performance are evident everywhere: in politics, economics, business, sports, recreation, law, parenting, education, and spirituality. Such also was the case in Keesta's day.

Orientation of the *Oosumich*

Keesta's *oosumich* for a whale hunt can be interpreted as a spiritually oriented ceremony. However, it is not to be taken in the same way that religious people pray to God for a supply of meat because such communication is between God and the petitioner, and the meat has no say in the matter. This is not a criticism of the latter method of petitioning; neither is it meant as a pejorative comment. Rather, it is a commentary about a difference in worldview. The latter worldview involves a communication system that can be highly effective between two types of beings, the human and the divine, while Keesta's worldview involves a communication system between three types of beings, the human, the animal, and the divine. This latter definition is useful only to a Western audience since a traditional Nuu-chah-nulth audience would not distinguish

Beach front at Nuu-a-such, known as Bartlett Island, a summer village site where Keesta landed his whales. The beach front looks out toward the Pacific Ocean.

between humans and animals in any essential, or spiritual, sense. Each definition is fraught with potential for misunderstanding because of radically differing worldviews that imply distinct meanings for the same words. In the Western sense, humans are biologically differentiated from animals. In a traditional Nuu-chah-nulth sense, human and animal biology are apparent manifestations of, and subsumed under, the reality of the hidden spirit realm, wherein lies the source of everything. Biological differentiation is not an issue from a Nuu-chah-nulth perspective. Scientific knowledge about biological processes is not an issue. Biological differentiation is acknowledged at one level of understanding. At another level of understanding, biological differentiation is understood as the result of transformations from a common source of being.

From my attempt to explain the Nuu-chah-nulth worldview, it will be correctly assumed that Keesta and his people were extraordinarily spiritual. Herein, however, lies another potential misunderstanding. Although the traditional Nuu-chah-nulth were extraordinarily spiritual in their daily lives, this spirituality was not exercised in the manner that Westerners might assume. Extraordinarily spiritual people in the Western sense are usually those who withdraw from society altogether and focus their lives primarily upon the unseen. They might become monks who

Views of Catface Mountain and of Nuchee (Mckay Island) from Ahousaht.
These are examples of sacred areas used by Keesta for *oosumich* purposes.

live alone and are otherwise divorced from the practical affairs of this
life. This type of spirituality presents a worldview based on a dichotomy
between the spiritual and physical. If one is spiritual in this sense, one is
not very much in touch with the earth.

Keesta's spirituality is summed up in the phrase coined by the Nuu-
chah-nulth members of the Scientific Panel for Sustainable Forest Practices in Clayoquot Sound, *heshook-ish tsawalk,* such that the spiritual

and physical form a single unified continuum (Bunnell and Atleo 1995). When the order of this continuum is understood, a picture emerges that may be alien to the prevailing views of a scientific world. It is a picture about an essential unity between spiritual and physical beings. Since the spiritual subsumes the physical in this order, all physical beings are the products of the spiritual. Although life is composed of an infinite number of physical beings, in the beginning all life forms were of one people, of the same essence. This commonality between species has not changed. In the anthropomorphic sense we are all related; we are all brothers and sisters not only to each other, but also to every life form. When values such as respect, kindness, generosity, humility, and wisdom are added to this worldview, Keesta's way of life may begin to make practical sense. The nature of creation as perceived by Keesta demands constraint and respectful protocols rather than brute, barbaric, and savage exploitation of resources. When a whaling venture becomes imminent as a result of consensual deliberation, a set of traditional family practices begins.

Decision Making

During the early 1940s Keesta's son Ahinchat (George Shamrock), who was by then my grandfather, would take me along to his councils. Although the Indian Act had forced the establishment of band council governance on reserves, during these years the traditional chiefs of the Ahousaht accepted these band councils as a form of bureaucracy subject to their ancient authority. Ahinchat and his councillors would sit in a circle and place each item, or issue, of an agenda into the middle of the circle. These councils were sharply focused on issues and their resolutions, rather than on the sorts of personal agendas that often complicate modern decision making. A major feature of this traditional process was the acknowledgment of every member of a council concerning each issue at hand.

While this decision-making process ensured every council member's input on every issue under discussion, it also required an unusual amount of patience, self-control, tolerance, trust, faith, and respect. Patience was required because of the likelihood that there would be a constant repetition of ideas. Every member had the right to speak even if that right meant constant repetition. Hence, whereas a modern meeting might address an issue in ten minutes, Ahinchat's meetings might have expended thirty or more minutes on the same issue. Although an observer of Ahinchat's meeting might have witnessed a focus on issues during the discussion, there was also an underlying focus that may have been more important. This underlying focus was the practice of respect for all life forms, the significance of which was that humans were given priority over process. It is more important to recognize the existence and value of people than to serve the process of decision making.

It was not necessary for each member to speak on an issue, but it was necessary to ensure that each understood the issue and that each had an opportunity to speak. When an issue was completely addressed and a solution seemed apparent, the process of repetition began again, with all members indicating whether they were in agreement with the proposed solutions. Sometimes an issue would invoke a unanimous and uniform response from each member of the council, whereas other issues would invoke differing and conflicting responses. These latter discussions would carry on in a respectful manner until every ambiguity and misunderstanding had been clarified and a decision could be reached.

Respect, as derived from a particular worldview that stands in opposition to the prevailing scientific worldview, is critical to the decision-making process. In Keesta's worldview every being is complete from the beginning. The completeness of creation, as conceived by a sacred or holy Creator, necessitates that all interactions between life forms be guided by respectful protocols. There is no room for any suspicion of genetic inferiority, for the idea that one species may be inherently inferior to another and must therefore be expendable. In Ahinchat's council all members treated each other with mutual respect. In practice this included the necessity not only of listening to diverse and conflicting opinions, but also of understanding these diverse opinions. If a council member of sound reputation suggested a solution that at first appeared ridiculous, too radical, or impossible in some way, he was not dismissed out of hand. Who knew, so the philosophy goes, whether the radical suggestion was not the result of some spiritual insight given to one council member and not to the others? Although common sense and logic played a major role in decision making, the council was also cautiously open to that valuable source of information commonly known in the Western world as intuition but known to the Nuu-chah-nulth as inspiration from a spiritual source.

Mutual respect in the practice of decision making is recognition that all humans are finite and that the most appropriate method of decision making must therefore be a unity of finite beings, two or more of whom working together, all things being equal, are greater than one finite being working alone. While most decisions were unanimous, others were not. In the case of a minority disagreement, it was usual for the conflict to be openly admitted. A case in point is a decision made by a traditional chief's council during the mid-1950s to build a recreational platform for children. The day following the decision, the community turned out in force to begin bringing in the small logs and lumber. One man was found working just as diligently as the other men of the community even though he continued loudly to disagree with the decision because he thought it was not workable. Now, had the project failed, one can imagine that there would have been a rise in community esteem for this one dissenter. As it turned out the project was a success, and the dissenter just as loudly proclaimed that, even though he had been against the project at the beginning, he could now see he was mistaken. This is an example of consensus decision making in which freedom of individual expression is retained in the context of a group-oriented society.

While the idea to engage in a whaling venture might originate with one individual, the chief, the decision to do so would proceed in the manner described above. Ahinchat would have learned this decision-making process from his grandfather Nokmis in the same way that I learned it from my grandfather Ahinchat. Once a decision has been made to engage in any venture, it cannot thereafter be directly discussed or referred to. No one would ever boast about a pending hunt lest the spirits of the hunted be alerted.

Unity of Purpose: Group Activity
The Nuu-chah-nulth have a deliberate but indirect manner of conversing that linguists have noticed. An example of an English transcription of this phenomenon might read as follows:

"What are you doing?"

"I'm making a spear."

"You must be about to engage in something big!"

"Yes!"

This manner of communicating arises directly from two conditions. The most immediate is the cultural cohesion created by a common language, values, and beliefs, whereby many things can be commonly understood. The season for whaling, a poor year for other resources such as salmon or seal or deer, the not unusual disappearance of men from the village for *oosumich*, the refurbishing of whaling canoes: all of these things might be in evidence, and thus everyone would recognize that preparation had begun for a whaling expedition. The relationship between making a spear and something big is never spelled out in specific terms. In this sense the Nuu-chah-nulth manner of conversing is a kind of code employed to prevent *others* (nonhumans) from understanding the meaning. *Others* in this case would refer to the intended target or targets. For example, if the spear was meant for sealing or for salmon, the code language would prevent the spirits of the seal and salmon from understanding the intent of the spear making.

The rationale for this belief that all beings not only have spirits, but can understand and communicate with one another, stems from origin stories that assume a common origin of life. Since all life forms share a common origin, it makes sense for all life forms to understand one another through their individual spirits. The physical and spiritual domains, as previously indicated, make up a single world, a single universe, a single reality. This state of existence, characterized by the common origin of all life forms and their interconnections, has given rise to the development of protocols of respect and constraint between all beings.

Spiritual Protocols

How the various life forms on earth should live together seems to have always been an issue. Among the Nuu-chah-nulth the tension between creation and destruction, wholeness and fragmentation, balance and imbalance, harmony and disharmony has been, over time, somewhat resolved. This has been achieved through acknowledgment and acceptance of the inherent polarity in creation rather than through its denial. The problems associated with the presence of evil – destruction by fire, earthquake, famine, disease, flood, sword, or predation – are balanced by the presence of good, manifested as creation, abundance, health, fine weather, peacetime, and safety from predators. In a moral universe full of a variety of interdependent life forms, relationships are conducted according to certain natural laws or protocols. These laws are explained in story. For example, there is a story in which Wolf pursues Deer, who has jumped high into a tree. As Wolf chops down the tree, Deer jumps into another nearby tree. This continues until Wolf begins to sing a supernatural song, at which point Deer's haunches begin to fall off one at a time. As the final haunch falls away and Deer comes tumbling down to his demise, he requests that his innards be treated in a specific, respectful manner. Even today both the wolves and traditional Nuu-chah-nulth hunters carry on this respectful tradition when a captured deer is being dressed.

Other stories tell of how to treat the great cedar and the salmon. These protocols are agreements between life forms. Their purpose is to ensure that life forms exercise mutual recognition, mutual responsibility, and mutual respect. To fulfill this purpose human life forms must recognize and respect their responsibility to other life forms. Nonhuman life forms will respond in kind. When mutual recognition, mutual responsibility, and mutual respect are practised, there is balance, harmony is achieved, and the goal of environmental and economic sustainability may be realized.

Ritual Cleansing and Prayer

On the west coast of Vancouver Island specific kinds of bushes or branches were used for the ritual act of cleansing. It is said that there is a certain kind of bush that, when used to scrub the body in fresh water, produces suds like a bar of soap. Ritual cleansing served a number of purposes. When applied to the body the act of ritual cleansing produces healthy physiological effects. Scrubbing with bushes or branches removes old skin, making way for new skin. In cold water, and in cold weather, the scrubbing stimulates blood flow to maximize nutrient distribution in the body. When accompanied by fasting, as it often is, ritual cleansing also allows the internal organs to cleanse themselves.

Another purpose of ritual cleansing would, today, be termed "character development." Ordinarily human beings tend to prefer the easy life and to eschew difficulties. The idea of sitting by a warm winter fire in the safety of one's own large house is much more appealing than the sometimes solitary privation of a mountain stream or mountain pool while exposed to the elements. It takes determination, courage, endurance, patience, and faith to spend time in a forest or on a mountain far from home, without food, warmth, or the company and security of relatives. Courage is especially required since it is known that existence is inherently dangerous. There are good powers, but there are also evil, destructive powers; who can know what will happen in a dangerous situation? On the other hand, ritual cleansing has been used successfully since time immemorial, and there is some satisfaction and confidence to be derived from this knowledge.

Another purpose of ritual cleansing arises from its relationship to body odour. Fasting, praying, and scrubbing vigorously with bushes or branches in cold water tend to eliminate or minimize human body odour. After several days of ritual cleansing, one test to determine whether human body odour has been effectively removed or minimized is to walk through your village at night to see whether dogs bark at you. Dogs, of course, have an exceptional sense of smell and are common to villages. Even more common are dogs barking at people during the night. If dogs bark at you, the entire cleansing ritual must be repeated until you can walk through the village without a single dog taking notice of your presence.

Smell is an important factor in the relationship between humans and other beings. Human odour, present in its natural form and force, may be attractive to other humans, but it may create a barrier against contact and communication with other kinds of beings. In a story about a chief who wishes to acquire spiritual power, human odour plays a large role in creating a barrier to effective contact. A wolf comes to this chief, who is lying down on the ground for the purpose of being captured, but the wolf does not carry him off because the human smell of the chief prevents it. After more effective cleansing, the chief is eventually carried off by the wolf. When the chief arrives in the wolf's home, all the wolves take off their cloaks and reveal themselves to be people. By eliminating or minimizing his body odour, the chief is able to make effective contact with the wolf people and, as a result, manages to acquire spiritual power.

A vital purpose of the cleansing ritual is to permit access to the spiritual realm through prayer. Prayer can be accompanied by the shaking of a rattle. Prayers are often uttered by chanting, and these have been called prayer songs. Some prayers are regarded as strong medicine and others as ineffective medicine. Strong-medicine prayers have positive outcomes, and ineffective-medicine prayers do not. Keesta preferred the former type of prayer.

In his preparations for a whaling expedition Keesta fasted, abstained from conjugal sex, performed ritual cleansing, and sang prayer songs over a period of eight months. He took with him the curled tail feather of a mallard duck. Since a curly tail feather does not uncurl under natural conditions, Keesta said that he would know whether his prayers were strong medicine when the curly tail feather straightened out of its own accord. Eventually the curly tail feather did just that, and only then did Keesta come down from the mountain. It is common knowledge not only in Atleo family history, but also among the older generation of the Ahousaht populace, that Keesta "captured" three whales in the traditional Nuu-chah-nulth way. The capture of these three whales can be attributed, from Keesta's orientation and testimony, to the efficacy of Keesta's prayers. The straightened tail feather was a supernatural sign indicating the tangible relationship between spiritual powers and physical powers.

Keesta was not only a whaling chief, but also an *ushdaxyu* (Nuu-chah-nulth doctor). He acquired medical knowledge about how to cure illnesses in the same way that he acquired knowledge about how to bring a great whale into his community in order to provide for its collective wellbeing – that is, by utilizing the *oosumich* method. Keesta's successful *oosumich* practice opened the storehouse of knowledge that is assumed to be common to both the spiritual and physical realms since both are creations of a single source: Qua-ootz. The foregoing claim is not necessarily a logical statement but an article of faith based on a worldview from which stem teachings and practices that have been affirmed by Nuu-chah-nulth community experiences since time immemorial. Keesta is one example of that community experience.

6 NUU-POOH

Tloo-utl-iss-sum Remember Me

When I became a young man and was able to go off by myself into the great world, my grandmother Margaret would always say to me as I left: "Tloo-utl-ee-sum." At the time I did not understand why she would want me to remember her in my travels. Now, in my later years, I can see the great theme that remembrance plays in the drama of life among the Nuu-chah-nulth. Every great ceremony demanded remembrance of who owned what, who had what name, who owned this dance and that song, who owned this *tupati* (spiritual power), where *hahuulthi* (ancestral territory) came from, and what we must do each day upon awakening: namely, remember Qua-ootz, Owner of All That Is, Owner of Reality. In your travels into different languages and cultures, remember me; don't forget where you came from; remember your roots, your rich heritage.

Ceremonial Expression

"Uh-chuckh [Who are you]?" an elder asked me on the Tofino wharf one day during the mid-1950s.

"Richard Atleo," I responded.

"No, no," he replied in English, "Who do you belong to, who is [sic] your father and mother?"

I was, at that time, living at the Alberni Indian Residential School while attending high school in Port Alberni. Although reasonably fluent in English, I was more comfortable speaking my own language, which was forbidden at the residential school. In fact, I never achieved the same level of comfort with the English language or with the dominant culture as I enjoyed with my own. Nevertheless, others noticed some changes in me. One day, on summer vacation as a teenager, while I was chatting happily in our own language, my aunt Flo said to everyone present, "Ah-uh-suhish mamamalthni qoo [He sounds like a white person]." This came as a shock to me and shook my confidence about speaking in my own language.

The question posed to me by the elder on the wharf in Tofino also shook my confidence. The influence of the dominant culture was affecting both the cadence, or accent, of my speech as well as my understanding of the nuanced meaning of Nuu-chah-nulth words. An extra syllable added to the elder's question would have specifically asked for my personal name, but without this syllable, "thluk," the elder was not asking for my personal name but for an indication of my lineage. Had I told the elder that I was the great-grandson of Keesta or the grandson of Ahinchat, he would have instantly been able to place me within my own community and its history and would have recognized my relationship to himself and his community. This story illustrates in part the phrase *heshook-ish tsawalk* (everything is one); it testifies that everything is interrelated and interconnected in the Nuu-chah-nulth worldview. While personal names are important in appropriate contexts, such as in interpersonal communications, Nuu-chah-nulth identity is characterized by an extensive lineage, together with its attendant history. Given an appropriate response, the elder who questioned me could have identified the *hahuulthi* (ancestral territory), the songs, and especially the stories of Keesta, who was recently deceased. As a close neighbour, the elder would have been familiar with rights to territory, names, dances, songs, *tupati* (spiritual power), and sacred ceremonies of every *hawilth* (chief) in that part of the Nuu-chah-nulth nation.

All aspects of formal life among the Nuu-chah-nulth, including matters related to sovereign rights over *hahuulthi* and its resources, together with names, prayer chants, songs, dances, *tupati*, and sacred ceremonies, are rooted in origin stories, the truths of which have been validated by *oosumich* and subsequently translated into the various cultural expressions found in the formal ceremonies of the potlatch. The Nuu-chah-nulth's ancient way of life still prevailed during the mid-1950s even though significant changes were becoming more evident. These changes were obvious not to outsiders but to insiders, to the Nuu-chah-nulth themselves. There was talk, during this period, of how to hold a cigarette properly, daintily between the thumb and forefinger. An attempt was made to get boys to pick up their dates from the girls' homes just as white boys did in the movies. It was just talk. People held their cigarettes in any way they chose, and no boy ever picked up his date from her house. For one, boys usually did not have money, and even if they did there was nowhere to spend it. For another, boys asking girls out on dates ran counter to the ancient practice of having parents decide which boys and girls should come together in marriage. This failure to change cultural practices in terms of boy-girl relationships, despite an express desire to do so, signals the depth, power, and continuing influence of the Nuu-chah-nulth's ancient values and life ways.

This chapter is based upon my lived experience in the traditional Nuu-chah-nulth community at Ahousaht during the 1940s, a decade prior to the encounter with the elder on the wharf in Tofino. It is an eyewitness account of a way of life that has been cut and pasted together in order to provide an insider's impression. It is a glimpse, not a comprehensive view, of an insider's perspective on a way of life that was, during and immediately after the Second World War, still primarily unaffected by the Western world and modernity. While Europe was having one of its many wars of the past two hundred years, the Ahousaht were enjoying 125 years of peace with neighbouring Nuu-chah-nulth communities.[1] While members of the powerful Western world were killing each other, the Nuu-chah-nulth were practising their ancient ceremonies, one respectful intent of which, it might be said, was to prevent destructive conflicts such as war.

All the names in the account are real, but they do not necessarily represent actual people of the time, the exception being those people mentioned in previous chapters, such as Keesta. The name and the description of the big house are authentic.

Location

Ahousaht is located on the sheltered side of Flores Island at the base of an isthmus that narrows to form a sheltered bay with a pebbled beach on one side and, on the other side, a sandy white beach facing the Catface mountain range. During the first half of the twentieth century, the housing layout of Ahousaht could be read as a map of the territory extending from Refuge Cove in the northwest down to Vargas Island and adjacent areas in the south and southeast. The Manhousaht branch of the Ahousaht lived on the northwest side of the village site, and the Vargas Island people, the Keltsmaht, lived on the southeast side of the village site. Each extended family, originally from a certain part of the confederated territory of the Ahousaht, lived in the village according to their geographic origins. The principal chiefs of the Ahousaht, for example, those who traced their ancestry to Ahous, lived appropriately in the centre of this community.

Although the federal Department of Indian Affairs had designated Ahousaht a reserve and encouraged an amalgamation of tribes for administrative convenience, the chiefs of the Ahousaht nevertheless maintained social and political control even when a system of governance based on elected band councils was introduced. During the time of Ahinchat, Keesta's son, the band council was conducted according to terms set not by the federal government but by the chiefs. The chiefs continued to exercise their political will over their *hahuulthi* (ancestral territory) and its resources. Advisors and counsellors who ordinarily attended to the chiefs became the band council's members and carried on business as before under the authority of the chiefs. No substantive changes took place in cultural life ways except that, for the purposes of Indian Affairs record keeping and official reporting to Parliament, the Ahousaht now had a modern, elective system of government. The band council, of course, did not have a budget itself. No one was paid except for the government's Indian Agent and his staff and the Indian Affairs mandarins in Ottawa.

The environment of Clayoquot Sound, as this general area has become known geographically, was relatively pristine at this time. There had been some logging but not to the extent of causing environmental degradation. Virtually all the historic salmon-bearing streams and rivers remained intact, teeming with coho, king salmon, sockeye, chum, and pink salmon. During the spring and summer months large schools of salmon were often reported off Kyuquot, Esperanza, Nootka Sound, Estevan, Raphael Point, Bear Island, Leonard Light, and down the length of Vancouver Island. In February and March the white milt of spawning herring could be seen in large quantities in all the inlets, channels, and bays as well as along parts of any sheltered shoreline. During the fall it was common for families to camp at traditionally owned river and stream mouths to dry and smoke salmon for winter supplies. Some technological changes, such as the use of modern clothing, motorboats, and Western household utensils had already taken place, but all these outward accoutrements had minimal impact on the inner person. The Nuu-chah-nulth, at this time, were still firmly in the grasp of their ancestral ways.

Sovereignty of Language

The best indicator of this continued adherence to ancestral ways was the preservation of the Nuu-chah-nulth language. During this period in Ahousaht, English was not a prevailing mode of communication any- where at any time. From the time one arose in the morning until it was time to go to sleep at night, the Nuu-chah-nulth language was the normative mode. Even Western foods and other Western items took on the flavour of the Nuu-chah-nulth language. Coffee became *qwapee*, chair became *chiya*, sugar became *shooqwa*, boat became *moot*, and any kind of sweet, including candy, chocolate, cake, pie, apples, and oranges, became *chamus*. *Chamus* means sweet food. Americans were not known as Americans but as Bostonahts because the original Americans to visit the West Coast came out of Boston. It did not matter to my grandmother whether visitors had come from Seattle or California or New York; they were Bostonahts. Americans, like all foreigners, were subject to a Nuu-chah-nulth designation, this being a practice befitting a people who still perceived themselves as sovereign. To my grandmother Margaret's dying day, the Americans remained Bostonahts, subject to the power of her ancient lineage.

In the scene that follows, it is the mid-1940s, and I am living with my grandparents. From this house I witnessed the dramatic call to come to an ancient ceremony and feast.

A Traditional Nuu-chah-nulth Feast

There is no wind, no sound, only a great silence in the village, filled with spiritual mysteries. A little boy is playing quietly on the beach side of his home. A large man walks toward the top of a small hill overlooking the beachfront and channel. The purposeful stride of the large man appears unusual in an otherwise unhurried community, alerting the little boy's keen sense. At the top of the hill the man stops and turns to face the west end of the village. As he fills his large chest with air, he tilts his head downward, his dark eyes piercing the far distance. His arms hang down, large hands clenched fiercely at his sides, and with dramatic formality he sounds the call throughout the land: "Yahts-shae-utl-ahhhhhhhhhh ... Ahoosaaaaaht! Yahts-shae-utl-ah [Start walking people of Ahous! Start walking]." This is an invitation for people to come to the feast.

It is a welcome sound and as exciting as any can be in human affairs. It is one way to sound an invitation to a local event. Another way is for *he-nah-tum-us* (emissaries) to go formally and ceremonially from door to door, loudly intoning the royal invitation at each. On this occasion, the feast is to be at Sutch-pee-ithl, the house of the head chief, Klee-kleeha. Next to Sutch-pee-ithl is Klaqkishpeethl, the house of Keesta.

Suddenly Ahousaht comes alive as people carrying their own utensils converge on Sutch-pee-ithl. The main entrance to Sutch-pee-ithl faces southwest, and two attendants are at the door. As little Cha-kwas-saqh-tin approaches, an attendant takes him by the hand and escorts him to a seat at the northwest end of the house. This is where the chiefs sit.

Five-year-old Cha-kwas-saqh-tin, from the house of Klaqkishpeethl, is an heir apparent and thus seated beside Ahinchat, his grandfather.

There are no tables or chairs in the main part of the great house but only wooden benches alongside the walls. At each end of the feast house are two iron barrel stoves. The stove in the southwest end stands alone and provides heat during feasts, while the one in the northwest end is for family cooking. There are two small windows on each side of the great house and a small one in an upper bedroom loft at the northwest end. After the fashion of the ancient big houses of precontact times, the house is made of wood, none of which is painted or finished. The introduction of new technology, which began slowly with the fur trade about 150 years earlier, has resulted in negligible change to the hearts of the Ahousaht even though its presence might suggest otherwise. The wood now comes from sawmills, the clothes come from factories, and to the diet have been added some new kinds of food, which are cooked on new iron stoves. Outside, a great, black, iron pot sits over an open fire. It is filled with rice and raisins for this occasion, but it could also be filled with meat or a variety of seafood on other occasions. The rice and raisins are not the main course but are meant as a treat. The main course comprises deer and elk meat, clams, sea urchin, fresh salmon, half-smoked salmon, seal meat, seal oil, bannock, the strong, tasty juices of the boiled water used to cooked the fresh and half-smoked salmon, and afterward some apples, oranges, pies, and cakes.

To the government's Indian Agents, missionaries, or officers with the Royal Canadian Mounted Police, who are occasionally present in the community, the various external changes to Nuu-chah-nulth technology, food, and ideas may appear to come to the fore in the Ahousaht's modern life ways. However, this is an illusion, a show, something of a circus or a pantomime for the benefit of the representatives of the colonial enterprise. During these visits by outsiders, ancient life ways are momentarily put on hold. All attention is focused on the visitor or visitors. Everyone becomes socially tense in the same way one becomes tense at an unfamiliar social gathering. As soon as the visitor or visitors leave, there is a little flurry of debriefing.

What did the agent come for? Why were the police here? When everyone has been sufficiently debriefed, the village resumes its ancient ways, its ancient pace. The visitors know nothing of this life way. To an outsider the children in the community are shy, which is to say that they are not forward with visitors. To an insider the children in the community are well trained, well behaved, and well taught. In their own cultural environment they shout and play and sometimes get into arguments and fights just like other children. To an outsider the people of the community are quiet, slow, and apparently know their place in the presence of white folk. To an insider the people of the community are respectful of all life forms, even life forms as strange as white folk. In the familiar comfort of their own cultural environment, they can be quick of wit, quick with a play on words, or as noisy as possible at a feast, loud teasing or bantering often taking place between men and women. Neither side has ever scored a decisive victory during my sixty-four years of observations. The women have always been equal to the men and sometimes just plain merciful toward them. But during this feast there are no visitors from the police, churches, or government, and traditional Nuu-chah-nulth life carries on.

All this food has been prepared in the homes of the relatives of the chief hosting the feast, as has always been done. All the seafood has come from the *hahuulthi* (ancestral territory) of the chiefs. It is the fall of 1944, and the other world is having one of its many wars of the twentieth century. Canada's constitution has made these ceremonial feasts illegal, but this prohibition is not presently enforceable because of the war. Except for one incident, when a Japanese submarine bombed Estevan Point (perhaps for target practice?), the Nuu-chah-nulth continued their lives relatively undisturbed. In some important legal and constitutional respects, this was somewhat of an illusion because most of the chiefs' *hahuulthi*, comprising land, rivers, lakes, mountains, and foreshore and offshore fishing areas, had already been effectively appropriated (a euphemism for "stolen") by the Canadian and provincial governments. In the meantime, the meanings of songs, dances, masks, curtains, prayer chants, genealogies, and declarations of *hahuulthi* were understood in the customary manner.

Once all the people have assembled in Sutch-pee-ithl, servers begin to distribute the food amid a general hubbub of festive conversation. Unlike at today's ceremonial feasts, there is no need here to be concerned about children running about and creating a disturbance. They are all well taught, trained, and disciplined to respect their parents, their beliefs, and their ancient ways. There is also no need to be concerned about language, for everyone is fluent in the Ahousaht dialect. English expressions are still unfamiliar and foreign to the ear despite half a century of missionary and settlement contact. Every word, syllable, intonation, and body movement is perfectly understood. Communication is easy, fluent, and harmonious. Close relatives smile broadly and greet each other with a range of relational noises, known as *ai-nawk*, which simultaneously blend cognitive and emotive communication. As the feast gets underway, a literal translation of some neighbourly dialogue might read:

> *(Inflected with warm relational sounds)* "Wiiks-haik-qwa [Is there nothing wrong with you]?"
>
> *(Blended with the same warm relational sounds)* "Ha-a. Wiiks-hai-shish [Yes, there is nothing wrong with me]."
>
> *(With relational intonations interspersed throughout the remaining dialogue)* "Soo-wa [And you]?"
>
> "Ha-a. Yu-qwa-shish wiiks-hai [Yes, there's nothing wrong with me too]."
>
> "Was-sutl-tlukh cha-coop [Where is your husband]?"
>
> "Haaa, nush-shitl-ish um-eekh-soo uk-ee [He had to go visit his mother]."
>
> "Ah-kinh [What's wrong]?"
>
> "Ti-ah-ah-tu-squi-ish [She must have fallen]."
>
> "Haaa, wiiks-hai wa-tus [Will there be nothing wrong with her]?"
>
> "Ha-a, wiiks-hai wa-tus-ish [Yes, there will be nothing wrong with her]."

After a time of eating and social catching-up between neighbours and relatives, some general bantering takes place, usually between men and women. The banter is loud, very public, and highly significant. There is no indication of gender inequity in these exchanges. The women do not cower nor lower their eyes or heads. Rather, they take action and vigorously defend their positions. There have always been some men and women at these feasts whose apparent role is to create general merriment. This might be done by loudly teasing someone about something that happened recently, as indicated in the following exchange:

> Upwah: I saw Mary *(who is a widow)* picking berries yesterday!
>
> Mary: Haa! *(suddenly wary of being put on the spot)* What are you saying?
>
> Upwah: I heard that you were picking them for John *(a widower)*. Isn't that right, John?
>
> John: Haa-uh! I've been waiting. I've been waiting for something sweet!
>
> Mary: Haa! I saw John picking berries too, but I didn't see any berries in his bucket! Why should I pick berries for him when he's already had his fill?

Throughout the feast, males make exaggerated noises (Aaaaahhhh) to signify that the food is extraordinarily tasty. Rather than be offended by such outbursts, the women who have prepared the food become flushed with satisfaction and pleasure. When a plate or bowl is empty a person may make tinkly noises with the utensils to tell the servers that more food is wanted. This action could be considered bad manners in the outside world, but here in a great feast hall it is encouraged. Sumptuous feasts reflect well upon the host chief's ability to provide for the well-being of his community. On these ceremonial occasions it is necessary and desirable to have more than enough food available. Overflowing feast tables are an indication that the host chief has been favoured with spiritual power. All useful earthly provisions are considered spiritual blessings.

After the people have eaten their fill, a large, barrel-chested man, trained in cold water from his youth, rises to his feet. He is the speaker for the host chief. He stands, motionless, in front of the southeast entrance, his cheeks painted with streaks of black ash to indicate the importance of the occasion. He wears no shirt. His dark eyes stare straight ahead, waiting for the general hum of conversation to subside. Then quietly, but with excellent voice projection, he begins: "Choo, hawiih, cha-cha-ma-daa. Na-ah-tuhh-utl-ich [Attention, chiefs, honoured guests. Listen all]." Slowly, the speaker for the host chief, in a voice as clear as that of a skilled bass baritone, begins to recount the genealogy and exploits, the lineage, wealth, and excellence, of the host's house. In translation the speaker's words may read thus:

> The one who has taken hold of you, invited you, brought you here, is our chief, Klee-kleeha. Now you see who he is. Klee-kleeha is his name. Everything he owns has come from his grandparents. He has great *hahuulthi* [i.e., a wide expanse of territory and resources]. The food that was set before you came from his *hahuulthi*. It was his grandparents who gave him his *hahuupa* [teachings]. It is because of these teachings that Klee-kleeha loves you. He is a chief who is in balance and harmony [with the environment, the people, and the universe]. You remember his grandfather, ancestor Klee-shin. He also loved you. He was a good chief. He also had everything. We were never in need with Klee-shin.

Then the speaker continues with the lineage of Klee-kleeha, pointing out his ancestors' greatness, their expanse of territory, and their many exploits.

Not an eye or ear in the house wanders. All pay rapt attention. Occasionally a loud "Eee-yo! [Hear! Hear!]" punctuates the air. Gradually, the crystal-clear voice rises in volume, gaining a momentum reminiscent of the way that swans might rise upward in graceful circles as they lift off from the waters until they are able to fly over the trees and thus escape the bay where they have been resting. As the volume of his voice rises, his great body leans forward and shakes with each emphatic word and phrase. His large right arm and hand punctuate the air. Finally, at the end of a resounding phrase, he pauses. The feast hall is silent except for the occasional flicker of noise from the fires in the iron stoves. Slowly, he lowers his arm. Slowly, he settles back on his heels. A dramatic pause. Then, again, he begins. His voice is a whisper that can, nevertheless, be heard to the back of the feast hall: "You are the essence of thanksgiving! You are the essence of thanksgiving! You have come here to push up against your chief [i.e., to support your chief]. You are all witnesses to what your chief is, to whom your chief is, to what belongs to him. Choo! It [this speech] is that long."

Several cathartic "Eee-yos! [Hear! Hears!]" can be heard throughout the hall. Now the host chief moves to stand beside his speaker, who begins to chant a prayer song. Four times the chant is repeated. The chant is owned by the host chief, who has many chants for different occasions. This chant is a prayer song of acknowledgment and petition – the acknowledgment of greater powers and a petition for favour so that all may go well. When he is finished there is another momentary pause. The air is charged. Then, from among the audience, an elderly lady stands up and responds. She too sings a prayer song that confirms, in spirit, the activity of the chief. Her song is a spiritual witness to a spiritual activity: spirit singing to spirit. For those in the feast hall the spiritual communication is heard and understood in the heart if not in the cognitive mind.

During this time there will be some preliminary gift giving to acknowledge some special guests. These may have recently suffered a loss to their family, and it is necessary to remember them during their official time of grief because they also remember you (by their presence) in your time of joy. Joy and sadness come together and somehow harmonize with one another, each supporting the other without contradiction. It is a classic example of *yaw-uk-miss*, the word for "love," which incorporates both the bliss and the pain of life, the agony and the ecstasy. Neither pain nor agony is eschewed in favour of love and ecstasy; both are embraced as necessary parts of reality. In this embrace of reality is a remembrance of Qua-ootz, Owner of Reality.

Tloo-qua-nah

All of a sudden the lights go out, leaving the feast hall in darkness. Wolves are heard outside, and the doors are made secure. Four times the wolves circle the feast hall, pounding on the outside walls. Then there is quiet, and just as suddenly the lights come back on. Security people begin to check the audience for children who may have been abducted by the wolves. Despite constant vigilance by each family, it is found that some children have gone missing. While the lights were out, the wolves stole the children by means of their supernatural power. The security people soundly reprimand the apparently negligent parents: "You must have forgotten the teachings of our grandparents; otherwise your children would not be missing."

This wolf ceremony is about mortal dangers. It is an ancient statement about the natural state of existence. If parents are not vigilant, strong outside forces may steal or lure their children away from the family and community. It has ever been so. It is still so today, except that now it is much worse. A strong outside force stole our children, who, over a few generations, became lost to their parents, lost to their heritage, lost to their ancestors, and lost to their people's teachings. However, if the community works together, it is possible to rescue these children who have been lost to their families and community.

The following morning, men appear as wolves on the sand beach of Maaqtusiis, the name of the village site of the Ahousaht people. The wolves are represented by certain *quus* (humans) who have inherited this role in certain families. Each man-wolf has a whistle made of a local wood, and the sound these whistles make is eerie. On the grass fronting the far side of the sand beach, a wolf camp has been set up. Reaching part-way down the sand beach from this wolf camp are several small trees that form a line. The wolves come out from among the trees and crawl around on the sand beach on their hands and knees. They do this four times. Their movements are deliberate, powerful, slow, and menacing. They are unafraid and thus strike fear into the hearts of the community. There is a stark unveiling of reality in their movements, the revelation of a truth that strikes at the core of being. Their ceremonial presence cries, "Whooooooo!!! Be careful!!! Life is dangerous. Be vigilant! Hold fast to the teachings of your grandparents!"

During this drama the Ahousaht community, which serves as a witness, keeps its distance on a small hill. At each appearance the wolves play with blankets by throwing them into the air. At each appearance some warriors advance to wrestle the blankets, which are symbols of identity, away from the wolves. The number of blankets equals the number of abducted children. While these blankets are in the wolves' possession, they control the cultural identity of their captives. This wolf ceremony is in accordance with ancient legends, which teach that all life forms share a common origin, or spirit: that of Qua-ootz, the Creator. What differentiates each is outward appearance, known today as biodiversity. Beneath the exterior appearance of the salmon, the bear, the wolf, the eagle, and the raven are people just like you and me.

Fortunately, the warriors are always successful in retrieving each blanket although each struggle is real and some struggles apparently dangerous. Once each blanket has been successfully retrieved, the wolves have no choice but to allow, although unwillingly, the abducted children to be returned to the community. Consequently, on the fourth appearance of the wolves, the captives must appear on the sand beach replete with ceremonial head and wrist bands made from tree branches. At this point the Ahousaht warriors advance for the final phase of the rescue. There is a physical struggle between the Ahousaht warriors and the man-wolves. Eventually, after much strife, great struggle, and evident mortal danger to the rescuers, the children are rescued.

During this time it is necessary to post sentinels at each corner of the village because actual wolves are also vitally interested in the proceedings. Although wolves disappeared from the West Coast for a period of time, they have since returned. If precautions are not taken, these wolves may attack members of the community conducting the ceremony (as happened in one instance). Proper preparation means adhering to strict physical and spiritual cleansing rituals.

What happens to the children during the period prior to their rescue and restoration to the community? In precontact times, if the wolves stole the son of the host chief, he was taken for a few days to a sacred place. This sacred place might have been an isolated beach or island, where a trusted uncle or other relative of the chief would instruct the boy in all the family secrets. If the wolves took some girls, they would be accompanied by female relatives to a secure place within the village and kept hidden until they were to be restored to their families. In modern times the abducted people are kept hidden from view in some local building.

In the meantime, the community members, who have been standing on the hill, advance to claim their loved ones who are being rescued. These loved ones are tied with a rescue rope that eager relatives can hold while escorting them back into the feast hall, back into the security of family and community. The children's abductions have brought trauma and devastation to the fabric of family and community. Now there is relief, a sense of joy, and anticipation of a great release of community power.

Before evening on the appointed day, the people reassemble in Sutch-pee-ithl for another feast. The air of the great feast hall now has a different charge. There is no loud public bantering. Instead there is expectation of a transformative event, of a great spiritual outcome. Once the feast is over the speaker appears in front of the curtain. His face is streaked with red on both cheeks. The children who have been rescued stand to the left of the speaker. The chief stands to the speaker's right, with his *hakum* (chief's wife) next to him on the outside. A victorious prayer song begins. Four times this spiritual prayer is lifted to the heavens. It is a celebration song, a song of gratitude and thanksgiving. The children were once lost and now are back in the family. Each will now get a new name to mark this special occasion. The chief will also assume a new name. It is a memorable occasion. The celebration of life may now begin under the auspices of the host chief. It is time for the community to rise to this occasion.

Accordingly, now is the time for a ceremonial response of acknowledgment, recognition, and respect from the assembled guests. Each family, in turn, sings a song, dances a dance, and makes a speech of recognition and thanksgiving to the host. Nuu-chah-nulth music and dance played a significant role in precontact life. Some of the first sounds heard by Captain Cook when he arrived at Nootka Sound were musical. The very first sounds heard would certainly have been prayer songs. It is a custom that precedes every undertaking, even today. The Nuu-chah-nulth were a prayerful people. Songs of identification indicating the sovereignty, power, heritage, and extent of wealth of the chief who owned the song would have followed the prayer songs.

Most songs were owned by someone. Each extended family had a bank of every variety of song: lullabies, joyful songs, love songs, prayer songs, gambling songs, and a host of other songs appropriate to an occasion. Those who engaged in whaling sang hundreds of songs related to various aspects of the venture. Those who engaged in sealing or in hunting for deer or elk would have songs to suit these activities. In fact, there were songs for almost any activity – for example, little songs for little children who fished for perch down at the docks. The Nuu-chah-nulth were so immersed in music and song that even little girls could spontaneously create a song about seagulls soaring gracefully in high winds, creating a dance for it at the same time. Seventy years later, my mother still remembers such a song and dance that she spontaneously created, with her girlfriend, while in school.

Men sang to themselves as they worked on carving out a fishing canoe or, later, as they worked on their modern, commercial fishing boats. Women sang to themselves as they worked around the house, mended clothes, or dried and smoked fish, and at night they sang lullabies to the children. Every mythical story told was accompanied by songs that were sung during the story telling. When Sawbill refused to marry Crane, Crane went to see Wren, who advised Crane to go to the top of Lone Cone Mountain, climb to the top of a tree, and sing the following song to the north, east, south, and west: "Naw-naw na-win sin-kee-ee. Clooputch ma-nin see-kee-ee [She said to me, she said to me. Let the seas rise, let the flood begin]."

Every child who has ever heard that story can see Crane standing on top of this tree, on top of this mountain, singing this song. Far to the south and west, the child can see the waters begin to rise, the waves rising high and lapping at the sides of this great mountain until it is covered in waves. The world is flooded and everything dies. Oh my! What a state! What happens next? Well, Crane sees that his revenge has been too great, so he instantly brings everyone back to life, no one realizing that they have just died. That's why, today, you can see Sawbill raising her young all by herself. Creation was not designed for the separation or alienation of individuals from one another but to emphasize togetherness and relatedness between life forms. Songs that accompany stories create an interest and excitement that appeal not only to the imagination, but also to the senses, to the soul, such that life becomes enriched and full.

The late Roy Haiyupis, from Ahousaht, told of a time when he was out hunting for deer around Vargas Island. He heard some faint sounds coming from nearby. As the sounds became louder he realized that it was the sound of singing. Roy laughed merrily at this memory because the old man who was singing was apparently also hunting for deer. Music played such a significant role in Nuu-chah-nulth life that it sometimes became overwhelming, in this case interfering with a hunting activity that required silence rather than music. Consequently, during a feast every family enjoyed the privilege of singing their songs and dancing their dances.

If a family has had a child abducted and rescued, they not only give a new name to their child, but also distribute gifts to the guests. Each gift is a thank you for attendance and for being a witness to an important occasion. Each gift accepted is a legal seal of approval. Every response to the host chief is an affirmation that may be expressed in the following words: "Yes, it is true Klee-kleeha has a great expanse of territory, great resources. He has a noble lineage. It can be seen that Klee-kleeha loves his people. The teachings of our grandparents are here with us today. This is what we are taught. This is the way we must be. Our spirits have become good. Our hearts have become glad. Praise be to Klee-kleeha."

At regular intervals during the ceremonies, young servers will bring refreshments around to the guests: tea, coffee, juice, and sandwiches, then oranges and apples. Sometimes, during a lull between performances by various tribal chieftains, a man may get up to dance the *kwee-qua-thla:* a very difficult but brief dance of pride and subtle skill in honour of the host chief. It is a dance of quick movements that coordinates the hands, feet, and face in such a way as to say: "I am full of joy, joy, joy." In a euphoric moment of oneness, of unity, of togetherness in the flesh and in the spirit, one person moves and articulates the pure joy of life, the *kwee-qua-thla.* When it is done well it is joy in motion. Every eye is fixed on the dancer, and every mouth is smiling. When the *kwee-qua-thla* comes to a sudden stop, the guests erupt, not with applause but with loud noises of approval from the throat: "Haah! Ah-tseek-ish-aw-nee [He is truly skilful]! Aw-nautl-ish ah-tseek [He really is skilful]!"

At other times various people from the community may "piggyback" on their host chief's ceremonial occasion by presenting a gift or gifts to friends and relatives. These gifts are not a direct expression of the present occasion but are meant to acknowledge friends and relatives who have been kind or helpful in a time of need. Often these people may not have the social or resource capital to host their own ceremony. A widow may present a gift to a family for helping her to move all her household goods from the city. A family may present a gift to one who rescued a family member whose fishing boat had broken down on the high seas. Each presentation is an affirmation of relationships, of interconnections in the web of life. The value of the gift is often not in its monetary value. A simple T-shirt or a handknitted sweater may serve to say "thank you" to a relative for taking in a whole family in the city when a loved one was critically ill or when a loved one was having a baby. Each accepted gift is an affirmation of the ancient *hahuupa* (teachings) to be kind, to be generous, to be helpful to those in need. Each accepted gift establishes the unseen but natural unity of existence. The family, community, and nation are strengthened through the visible and concrete act of gift giving because the giver and receiver are brought closer together through a common life experience.

Often, in the midst of all the ceremonial activity, a family may get up and announce a feast to be held in the village six months or a year hence in honour of a marriage or of some accomplishment or momentous event in a person's life. Everyone is invited. Thus the ceremonial life carries on without an obvious written policy, without an obvious written constitution for guidance. The ceremonial feasting activity has been going on for millennia, taking care of every human need, politically, socially, economically, and spiritually. The guidance, of course, is woven into the mythic fabric of origin stories, those of Raven, Wolf, Deer, Wren, Bear, Salmon, and many more of Qua-ootz's creations, and complemented by *hahuupa* (teachings) and the ancient customs of cleansing, fasting, and prayer that accompanied the exploits of ancestors.

When all the immediate ceremonial needs of the community have been met, when every family has had an opportunity to respond to the host chief, he rises once again to conclude the ceremonies. His speaker stands next to him and begins a prayer song of thanksgiving, which is sung four times. In the meantime, two dancers who have been preparing for this moment wait behind the curtain.

Suddenly a man takes a determined three or four steps onto the main floor. He has come from among a group of singers who are standing in a circle at the east end of the feast hall. Singers usually sit in a circle for most songs, but they stand for sacred songs that belong to chiefs. This man is like the herald of a king, or chief, and he shouts to the assembled at the top of his voice: "Wa-moss soo-taaaaaallllth! Nook uks clah oo ye! Nook uks clah oo ye [Speak I to yooooooou all! I have a song, right now! I have a song, right now]!"

Immediately a lone voice rises from the lead singer of the group, who is now standing in honour of, and respect for, the sacred meaning of this song and dance. It is an introductory chorus to a sacred *hinkeets* (bearing gifts) song of the host chief. As the introduction to the song is completed, there is a musical pause. Then a thunderous sound of ten drums fills the air. As the rest of the singers join the song, a *hinkeets* dancer with a wolf's headdress appears at one side of the chief's curtain, which hangs thirty feet across one end of the hall. The curtain is a postcontact innovation created in response to the oppression of Aboriginals inherent in the Indian Act, which forbade such ceremonies taking place. During precontact times wooden murals were used for such occasions. These were painted with designs belonging to the chief.

Hinkeets dancers Taras (left) and Shawn Atleo, sons of the author, performing at Thunderbird Hall, November 1986. Shawn, whose chiefly name is Ahinchat, is the family *taises* and current holder of the Atleo seat.

When the potlatch was outlawed it was difficult to hide these murals if the police or a missionary showed up unexpectedly. Curtains, on the other hand, are easy to fold up and put away.

Now the guests await the grand finale to their host chief's feast. A chief's attendant stands beside the crouched dancer, who wears a black cape adorned with significant designs derived from a spiritual dream or vision. At the right moment in the music, the chief's attendant imperceptibly waves this first dancer onto the floor. The dancer twirls in a counterclockwise direction and, with wolflike movements of the headdress, begins to dance parallel to the curtain. He is young, strong, from the chief's family, and wears no shirt under the cape. He is naked except for modern shorts. He dances, lifting his feet in rhythm with the drumbeats, moving the headdress from side to side. When he is part-way across the dance floor, the chief's attendant waves the second *hinkeets* dancer onto the floor. His cape flashes through the air as he twirls in a counterclockwise direction.

The *hinkeets* dancers must listen to the instructions of the song leader. Some dances demand a sudden and dramatic interjection, which requires a change of musical beat and dance movements. When such a change is required, the song leader will warn the dancers. At the sound of warning, the *hinkeets* dancers may stop dancing momentarily in order to position and prepare themselves to perform the extraordinary moves soon to be demanded. One such change requires that the *hinkeets* dancers twirl rapidly in 360° circles on the spot, first counterclockwise and then clockwise, for a period of four musical lines. At the end of these four lines, a musical pause unites the whole community and serves as a transition back to the original 4/4 musical time.

This interjection is called *empt-empt-ta,* which means to name. It has a correlation to the chorus in Western songs. The main parts of the *hinkeets* song are sung four times, and normally the series of 360° twirls is performed once, except when the song and dance have an extraordinarily powerful effect on the spirit. In such a case the song leader will shout *who-a-tsa-a-pee,* the literal meaning of which is "put it back to where it was." In translation the phrase can be interpreted as "sing it again!" When the dancers hear these instructions, they know that the singers will sing one verse before returning to the chorus again. Accordingly they will momentarily stop their dancing and position themselves for the 360° twirl.

Whenever a song leader shouts the instruction *who-a-tsa-a-pee* (sing the chorus again), it signifies an inspirational moment that speaks volumes about the host and all the preparations. It is normal for the host chief and close members of his household to be spiritually prepared long before the onset of a ceremonial feast. In addition, those families who have been planning to attend and perform their songs and dances must also be prepared. The inspirational moment signifies the prevalence of good spiritual powers over other powers that might seek to disrupt and disturb. The inspirational moment is also a harbinger that the general outcome of this ceremony will be beneficial, that every protocol of respect demanded of ceremonial feasts will be fulfilled. The host chief is recognized by good attendance and enthusiastic participation. The singers, dancers, family speakers, cooks, servers, security, chief's attendant, master of ceremonies, prayer chanters, and every family who contributed are *ha-mutt-shitl* (made visible/publicly recognized). All are associated with spiritual power through its demonstration during the ceremonies and feasting.

These ceremonies are strongly focused on the importance of relationships, of maintaining protocol, of showing respect, and of demonstrating these attributes through the generosity of food, gifts, and relational oratory. Relational oratory emphasizes not only kinship ties, but also the accomplishments or acts of significance attributed to the subject.

When people find the ceremonial feast of the host chief to be inspiring, the relational oratory takes on euphoric tones, and young servers happily and often playfully distribute sandwiches, oranges, apples, and other fruit to the guests. The feast hall is charged with a sense of community wellbeing, which is the context for *who-a-tsa-a-pee:* Put it back to where it was; sing and dance it again! It is then that the singers, male and female dancers, and guests come together in one relational unit, fulfilling *heshook-ish tsawalk* (everything is one), an inherent characteristic of creation as conceived by Qua-ootz, Owner of Reality, Creator and God.

Flanking each side of the dance floor are female dancers, each wearing a black cape. Rhythmically they twirl back and forth on the spot, maintaining a protective formation that encloses the *hinkeets* dancers. It is a sacred dance, and whenever it is made visible or publicly performed, it is a challenge to destructive spiritual powers. The *hinkeets* dance is a dance of spiritual power owned by a chief who requires this kind of power in order to provide for the wellbeing of his people. When the song and dance are concluded, there is no applause even if the air is charged with inspirational euphoria. This Western custom has not yet been learned. Instead, if the song and dance has been particularly inspired, there will be shouts of praise and approbation: "Why-kosh itsk Hawilth! Why-kosh itsk [You are to be praised! Chief! You are to be praised]!" Immediately the speaker will step onto the floor and ceremonially proclaim: "Tsee-thlooo! [A public announcement of a ceremonial gift] Chief Ah-up-wha-eek (who is the highest ranking guest chief on this occasion)."

Upon receipt of this public gift for being a witness to all the claims of the host chief, Ah-up-wha-eek will respond with "Tlecooo! Tleco [Thank yooou! Thank you]!" Ah-up-wha-eek, and his entire house, are now party to an agreement represented by the ceremonies of this feast. The history of Klee-kleeha, the host chief, is confirmed and substantiated. The genealogy and *hahuulthi* (ancestral territory) are affirmed and ratified. Subchiefs and other important people may receive less, but each gift, including the gift of feast food, signifies a confirmation and affirmation of the claims of the host chief.

If the host had been from the house of Klaqkishpeethl, the guests may have witnessed the use of the *chu-chalth:* a song and dance that was performed by Keesta's family because of his marriage to Queen Mary, who, in the absence of a male heir, held the chief's seat (chief of the Keltsmaht). The *chu-chalth*, which refers to the dorsal fin of a whale, is a sacred dance led by the chief's wife or close female relative that was originally performed to welcome the whale to the beach and to pay it honour.

Now it is used as an opening ceremony, and every time the *chu-chalth* is performed it represents and references a magnificent heritage that embodied a meaningful understanding of the state of existence. Whales are not a commercial commodity in this understanding; they are great personages who require great respect and an appropriate ceremonial recognition for their important role in the mysteries of life. The *chu-chalth* today is a testament to the exploits of a generation of Nuu-chah-nulth who lived to see a twentieth-century world that did not know of this song and dance, much less understand its significance.

Originally the general outline of events related to the successful capture of a whale by Keesta would have begun with an orderly and customary distribution of the whale meat. The distribution of the whale meat by Keesta to a Nuu-chah-nulth community fulfilled a chiefly responsibility. The measure of provision was proportional to the measure of esteem in which a chief was held. The more successful – that is, the more spiritually powerful – a chief proved to be in providing for the wellbeing of his community, the greater the measure of esteem for the chief. There is much room for misunderstanding in this discussion. For Keesta there was no dichotomy in his worldview between things spiritual and things physical. There was a direct correlation between the capture of a whale and spiritual power or spiritual blessing. The whale meat was a manifestation of spiritual blessing and thus similar to manna from heaven in Keesta's worldview.

The implications of this worldview were far-reaching. The esteem in which a great chief was held by his people was experienced in the context of spirituality. People found great joy and reverence in their direct or indirect connection to someone who had a close relationship with Qua-ootz, the Creator. The closeness of Keesta's relationship with Qua-ootz was evident in the favour that Qua-ootz bestowed upon him. For this reason, the Spanish explorer José Mariano Moziño concluded that Chief Maquinna's role, in part, was like that of a high priest. According to Moziño's understanding of reality, Maquinna interceded between God and people. However, it is not clear that a Nuu-chah-nulth vision quest can be interpreted as an intercession even if the quest appears to be an exact replica of intercession in its difficulty, danger, discipline, and testing of human endurance. The intention of the vision quest and the intention of Western spiritual intercession may be identical – that is, the attainment of spiritual gifts or assistance – but the underlying rationale may not be the same.

Intercession arises from a worldview premised on the idea that God is angry and thus demands to be appeased by sacrifice. The vision quest arises from a worldview premised on the idea that Qua-ootz and the life forms of creation must live together in mutual recognition, mutual responsibility, and mutual respect. The same difficulties of existence are present in both worldviews, but they are perceived in different ways. In the first view, creation is at fault, necessitating intercession for the wellbeing of the community. In the second view, difficulties are considered inherent to creation rather than something to be complained about. Certainly, difficulties appear, in this view, to be part of ongoing acts of creation such as the traditional Nuu-chah-nulth acts of finding, accessing, cutting, shaping, burning, carving, and then transporting out of a forest a newly made canoe that was once a great cedar tree. In this sense difficulties help to create and define a personally purposeful existence that humans have a responsibility to discover.

In the present case, the ceremonial expression of the *tloo-qua-nah,* "we remember reality" or "we remember the Owner of Existence," helps to remind us of two important facts about the original design of creation. One, the "we" who remember reality is all-inclusive of life forms. In this view of existence, survival-of-the-fittest and natural selection do not apply because everyone, without exception, has a place, a purpose, a reason for being. Two, although the difficulties of existence are necessary to creative acts, they can also serve to destroy. Consequently, recognizable and bounded units of existence, such as a family or community or nation, must always be in a struggle to continually overcome difficulties that may not only hinder but threaten to destroy.

Ceremonial Conclusion
After the last song has been sung, the last dance performed, and the last gift distributed, one more event remains. Since there has been a great variety of songs, dances, speeches, and gift giving over an extended period of time, it is useful, necessary, and respectful to refocus the entire festivity upon the host. To this end, before anyone leaves the great feast hall, a man of rank strides to the centre of the hall. To the Western eye this act may seem presumptuous because anyone who stands in the centre in the Western world demands attention for the purpose of self-aggrandizement. However, to the Nuu-chah-nulth eye the act is recognized as one of humility and respect because the man does not stand where the great chief has stood on all ceremonial occasions – that is, at

115

one end of the feast hall. Moreover, the act does not honour the man but the host chief.

Once again, there is a summary of the great lineage and largesse of Klee-kleeha. Unlike the modern world, which regards ancestors as living in the past, the Nuu-chah-nulth culture perceives *na-na-nikx-soo* (ancestors) as living in the present. They may not be here in the flesh, but they are always here in spirit. For this reason, they are always acknowledged as contributors to any ceremonial occasion. Their teachings, their ceremonial practices, their exploits, and their presence all affirm *heshook-ish tsawalk* (everything is one). The *tloo-qua-nah* has been an enactment of this reality. It contains danger. It contains pain and sorrow at the loss of loved ones. It affirms the frailty of *quus* (humans), who are unable to be perfect. Lastly, it affirms Qua-ootz, Owner of Reality, who – when remembered and approached in a manner consistent with the principle of humility taught by Son of Raven – is able to help *quus* safely restore lost loved ones to community.

7 UTL-POOH

Heshook-ish Tsawalk Everything Is One

Nuu-chah-nulth origin stories and traditional Nuu-chah-nulth life ways and experience indicate that the basic character of creation is a unity expressed as *heshook-ish tsawalk* (everything is one). This unity of existence does not mean that individuals are denied a separate existence; on the contrary, individualism is a very strong value. *Heshook-ish tsawalk* is a matter of the first principles laid out in the original design of creation. The Creator and creation are one. Within this metaframework of existence are the contemporary universe of quantum mechanics, superstring theory, philosophies and political ideologies, biodiversity, and every expression of life known and unknown.

Theory of Tsawalk

Although, from the perspective of lived experience, this view of creation is ancient, from a theoretical perspective it is very much emergent. My theory appears to be similar, even identical, to some contemporary theoretical ideas that employ the concept of *context* in social science and environmental discourses. However, important assumptive aspects of my theory differ sharply from any Western theory. In my earlier research into student outcomes in a variety of contexts over time, I originally conceived of Tsawalk as a theory of context. In one respect, context defines recognizable units of existence, such as age group, gender, home, school, geographical region, society, and heritage, but Tsawalk, by comparison, also refers to the nonphysical and to unseen powers. Consequently, because the theory does not exclude any aspect of reality in its declaration of unity and, most important, because the concept of *heshook-ish tsawalk* demands the assumption that all variables must be related, associated, or correlated, I now call this view of reality the theory of Tsawalk.

Whereas the methodologies of the physical sciences demand the isolation of one or two variables so that cause and effect can be measured, the theory of Tsawalk assumes that any variable must be affected by a multitiude of additional variables that can be found in a variety of contexts across different dimensions of experience. In social science research this assumption means that any individual is necessarily subject to such variables as family of origin, geographical region, social status, genetic inheritance, local and global economic conditions, politics, spirituality, and other recognizable units of existence, each of which has a varying degree of influence in determining the make-up of an individual, who may be a successful professional or an alcoholic or a combination of both.

This aspect of Tsawalk does not challenge or call into question the methodologies of the physical sciences, but only implies that they are founded on a perspective of existence that differs from the alternative perspective suggested by a worldview wherein the universe is regarded as a network of relationships. While any scientific study, from any theoretical perspective, including that of Tsawalk, may find a statistically strong relationship between variables, it is also the case that other relationships may prove to be very weak. However, because the theory of Tsawalk assumes reality to be *one* network of relationships, it may also be assumed that even if a variable does not show a strong statistical relationship to other variables in one study, this same variable must, by definition, reveal a set of variables to which it does have a strong relationship in another study. Consequently, where variable D is found not to be significantly related to variable A, variable D must have its own set of variables, say E, F, G, and H, to which it is significantly related.

That the theory of Tsawalk holds different assumptions about the universe from those held by many Western theories means that any methodological approach developed according to the principles of Tsawalk will demand more rather than fewer variables for any given study. Known statistical measurements can still be applied, but new ways of measurement will likely have to be developed to reflect the dynamics of a universe composed of a network of variables in a network of relationships.

The scope of Tsawalk's theoretical applications can range from investigations into the metaphysical to investigations into both the natural and social sciences. These areas of study are introduced by a discussion of *oosumich* as a Nuu-chah-nulth research method.

Oosumich as Nuu-chah-nulth Methodology

The metaphysical, or spiritual, domain of existence is not yet a main-stream area of research. Nevertheless, Nuu-chah-nulth origin stories, upon which the theory of Tsawalk is based, clearly show that the physical and spiritual domains are intimately related. In the same way that Raven and his community utilized the *oosumich* method to explore the nature of the spiritual-physical relationship, it is possible to employ the theory of Tsawalk to continue this exploration within a contemporary academic setting.

Initially this may require that the contemporary and *oosumich* research methods be applied independently, but it may eventually be possible to combine the two approaches. Their differences may be monumental, but the two methods are not necessarily incompatible. *Oosumich* is a spiritual method, while contemporary research methodologies are based in the physical domain. Both methods have their own ways of establishing and verifying fact. *Oosumich* and contemporary research methodologies are like two different cultures with two distinct languages and ways of life that are currently not mutually understandable. However, one implication of the theory of Tsawalk is that the methodologies of *oosumich* and contemporary research belong together, these being two proven methods of acquiring verifiable information. Since *oosumich*, as a Nuu-chah-nulth method of knowledge acquisition, is modelled in principle after the method employed by Raven and his community, it is necessary to summarize some of the important features of the story.

In the story of How Son of Raven Captured the Day, one community is of the earth, while the other community is of the spiritual domain. A relationship between the two communities is assumed not only by Raven and his community, but also by those in the spiritual realm. In fact, it appears that the Wolf community in the spiritual realm has always been aware and expectant of the earth community. When Deer attempts to escape with the fire attached to his tail, the Wolf community is not taken by surprise. Deer is not able, despite his agility and speed, to escape even the confines of the dance floor. When the earth community transforms itself into salmon, the heavenly community keeps a sharp lookout for any unusual activity from the earth. Thus, when Raven turns himself into a giant king salmon rather than into the smaller sockeye salmon, this unusual mix within a school of salmon instantly alerts the heavenly community. Likewise, when he assumes the form of a giant salmonberry shoot, he is detected. Each earth strategy fails until Raven is advised to transform into an insignificant leaf. What a blow to a monumental ego. The boastful mentality evident in Raven's transformations into a giant king salmon and a giant salmonberry shoot is reduced to a liability.

In this story the process of making a meaningful connection between earth and heaven is the real challenge, not the connection itself. The connection, the relationship that is assumed to be inherent in the nature of existence, is not the challenge in this story. The only real challenge is to discover what kind of relationship works. When Raven is eventually born into the Wolf family, the nature of the relationship between the spiritual and physical domains becomes evident. Heaven and earth are so closely related that it is possible for a physical being to be born again as a spiritual being. This correlation between the spiritual and physical domains represents an astonishing degree of intimacy. Not only are these apparently disparate realms connected, but they are also intimately related. Raven, the son of earth, becomes a son of heaven, a son of the Creator, Qua-ootz, Owner of Reality. Raven's actions comprise not a creation, but an unveiling, of such a relationship, a revelation of that which is inherent in the design of creation: *heshook-ish tsawalk* (everything is one).

This is precisely the point! Raven assumes that there is a relationship between heaven and earth and, together with his community, sets about discovering what makes the relationship work. Without this assumption about the relationship between the two apparently disparate realms of the physical and spiritual, Raven and his community might just as easily have given up and concluded that no such relationship exists. Many who are agnostics can come to such a conclusion, while atheists may deny any spiritual existence at all.

The story of Raven is an example of investigations into the metaphysical. The methodological approach to knowledge and power acquisition implied in the story of Raven's capturing the light can be likened to a research paper. First, a problem is identified: People are in need of light. Second, theories are developed about how the light may be obtained. Third, methodologies are developed and strategies devised, from the king-salmon approach to the tiny-leaf approach, with which to test the theories. Fourth, data are collected through actualization of the strategies. And, fifth, a strategy's successful execution is understood as lending some credence to the theory that together the physical and spiritual domains comprise a meaningful unity of existence.

Countless thousands of these *oosumich* research papers, metaphorically speaking, have been experienced and witnessed throughout the ages. *Oosumich* is the Nuu-chah-nulth equivalent of a vision quest. Raven's successful interaction with the owners of light, the Wolf community, is replicated among the Nuu-chah-nulth through the spiritual methodology of *oosumich*. Replication of this type of research is, in the first instance, neither a community nor a national responsibility but a personal one. The principle of personal responsibility is the same in scientific research. A scientist may work alone for years until a breakthrough is made, at which point the research outcome is disseminated through papers, publications, and conferences. *Oosumich* may be done for years until something highly significant occurs that affects the whole community, and only then is the outcome conveyed in songs, dances, and appropriate ceremonial displays.

The story of Keesta, some of which is recounted in Chapter 5, is one example among countless other Nuu-chah-nulth stories concerned with the successful practice of *oosumich*. The curly tail feather that straightens out of its own accord, as a sign of answered prayer, is not unusual in Nuu-chah-nulth experience. The heavenly intervention through the personage of Wren, who landed on the whale with a message for Keesta, is a measure of the complexity in the spiritual-physical interface. The final outcome in Keesta's story is the capture of a great whale that helps to provide for the wellbeing of Keesta's community. One may wonder, given today's material-focused age, and its attendant egotism, how Keesta was able to employ the insignificant-leaf approach in his dealings with heaven. When Keesta was growing into manhood and approaching middle age, the full impact of the materialistic age had not yet been felt in his village.

The rituals enacted by Keesta seem to have been standard practices around the world among indigenous people, including the Hebrew people of the Old Testament. Common are ritual cleansing, fasting, isolation from human society, prayer, petitions, and waiting until an answer is received, a sign is given, a definite connection made. The process can be described as paying attention to spiritual matters while intentionally ignoring earthly matters such as food, physical comfort, and social contact. Among the Nuu-chah-nulth, *oosumich* was a universal practice well into the twentieth century. Even today, some (if not many) still practise *oosumich*. It has always been, and still is, practised in secret, which is why even some modern Nuu-chah-nulth are unaware that it remains very much alive. This feature of the *oosumich* may also explain why it may be difficult to marry it with contemporary research practices.

As Son of Raven is an archetype of the ideal relationship between heaven and earth, between a created person and the Creator, Keesta modelled himself after this archetype. However, many other kinds of relationships can exist between the physical and spiritual domains. At the negative end of creation's spectrum, Aulth-ma-quus represents another archetype: that of an evil, destructive person who possesses overwhelming power over earthly beings. Consequently, the theory of Tsawalk can predict that existence is inherently subject to creative and destructive powers of varying degrees. This assertion is quite different from the philosophical notion that negative powers are mere creations of human beings, that without humans, negative powers would not exist. Neither is this an assertion that negative powers existed before creation. It is simply a proposition about postcreation existence that is accepted without question, a mystery.

The account of the Anglican priest Andrew Ahenakew in the introduction to this book represents the positive, creative end of the spectrum in the spiritual-physical interface, while a mass murderer would represent the negative, destructive end of this same spectrum within creation. One is dedicated to helping and healing, while the other is dedicated to death and destruction. Both powers have been ever present in the Nuu-chah-nulth's lived experience.

Since Qua-ootz is the Creator, it must be assumed that the spiritual domain is the source of the physical domain. This assumption is the context for the story of Raven, which in turn is a model for the effective practice of *oosumich*. When *oosumich* is practised using the insignificant-leaf approach – that is, from an earthly stance of humility toward Qua-ootz – the theory of Tsawalk predicts that petitions for food or power or gifts can be successful. The kind of power or success acquired will be consistent with both the goodness of the petitioner's intent and the good character of Qua-ootz, rather than with the evil, destructive character of Aulth-ma-quus.

This is clearly suggested in the sacred ceremony known as the *tloo-qua-nah*. The *tloo-qua-nah* reminds the Nuu-chah-nulth that *heshook-ish tsawalk* (everything is one) and includes both creative and destructive powers. Just as Raven is an archetypal human so too is Wolf an archetypal heavenly personage who represents creative power. A community of these wolves forms the archetypal heavenly community in the same way that angels form the heavenly community in Christian stories. The Wolf chief is an archetype of the Creator, the Almighty, Qua-ootz, Owner of Reality. The Wolf ritual is a constant reminder of the natural intimacy between heaven and earth, between the spiritual and physical realms.

The very name *tloo-qua-nah* means "remember-reality-we." Since one of the Nuu-chah-nulth names for the Creator is Qua-ootz, Owner of Reality, the wolf ritual becomes a constant reminder of the relationship between Creator and created. Good and evil flow constantly between the spiritual realm and the earth. The ritual abduction of children in this ceremony represents the evil, while the rescue and restoration of these children to the community represents the good. When the ritual abduction takes place, the parents of the children who are being *tloo-qua-nah(ed)* are ritually chastised in the public forum of the feast hall. It is loudly proclaimed that: "Your children are missing! You parents have not been appropriately watching over your children. You must have forgotten the teachings of our grandparents."

Fortunately, the earth's inhabitants, the Nuu-chah-nulth among them, are not left to their own devices against powerful destructive forces from the spiritual realm. The antidote resides in *hahuupa* (teachings). Children are lost to community because of a lapse in teachings by parents. They can be rescued through *oosumich* and the remembrance of Qua-ootz, the author of *hahuupa*. There, on a hill in the village, the community gathers in constant prayer while rescue attempts are made by brave warriors. The prayers are heard and answered. The warriors, after the fourth appearance of the wolves on the beach, successfully rescue the children. During the rescue the community moves in to help the warriors as they lead the children back to community and into the feast hall. Together they perform extended ceremonies, rituals, prayer chants, sacred songs, and dances in joyful remembrance. In traditional precontact times these ceremonies might have extended to twenty-eight days, a full cycle of the moon.

Application to the Metaphysical

Since traditional Nuu-chah-nulth practitioners can collectively testify to the efficacy of the *oosumich* method of knowledge and power acquisition, it may now be time to verify this data bank of indigenous knowledge using contemporary academic research methodologies. A virtually endless array of research questions can be devised to examine the metaphysical: Can the Nuu-chah-nulth data gathered through the practice of *oosumich* be classified? Do some spiritual experiences require more effort than others? Under what conditions are creative spiritual forces stronger than destructive forces? How much of the effectiveness of traditional medicines acquired through *oosumich* is attributable to the chemical substances found within medicinal plants, and how much of this effectiveness, if any, is attributable to the power of belief? Are there some powerful medicinal secrets obtained through *oosumich* that the *ushdaxyu* (medicine person) is not allowed to disclose? What, if any, are the reasons for nondisclosure? Can anyone pray effectively? What criteria might determine the effectiveness of prayer? How can the power of prayer be measured? Can this power be indicated by the chemical changes that take place in the brain under certain controlled emotional or spiritual conditions? Can the chemical profile of the brain of people engaged in *oosumich* be compared to the chemical profile of people who are not thus engaged? It is true that some of these questions have already been subjected to scientific investigation, but the *oosumich* method may provide additional, corroborative, or even new information in the field.

Of greater interest to physicists might be the question of whether the methodology of *oosumich* might be helpful in their investigations into the world of electrons, protons, neutrons, and quarks. The reception of information via *oosumich* is not subject to physical limitations common to scientific investigations because a person may leave his or her physical body and travel and observe by means of the human spirit. Whereas electrons are necessarily invisible to the human eye, they are not necessarily invisible to the human spirit through the practice of *oosumich*. Of equal interest to scientists in this discussion of relationships that may be found in the spiritual-physical interface are the limitations of human cognition, those necessarily imposed by a physical brain. If the spiritual domain is the source of the physical domain, it may follow that *spiritual cognition*, if you will, can enable one to circumvent the limitations of physical cognition. The first step will be to determine that there is a spiritual cognition apart from, yet underlying, physical or human cognition. In turn, perhaps through the practice of *oosumich* methodology, a way can be found to test whether spiritual cognition is able to expand physical cognition, each being intimately bound to the other in a manner consistent with the theory of Tsawalk. A proposition based on the theory would postulate that the greater source of intelligence is not physical but spiritual. This order of creation does not imply that humans are puppets but simply that humans are a secondary order of life, of intelligence. The practice of *oosumich* is an acknowledgment of the cognitive limitations of the physical domain.

Application to the Natural Sciences

In its assertion of the unity of all things, the theory of Tsawalk has been affirmed in the physical universe by quantum mechanics. The same proposition has been affirmed by students of the environmental sciences, wildlife biology, fluvial morphology, forest ecology, ethnobotany, and marine biology, and by representatives of related disciplines who sat on the Scientific Panel for Sustainable Forest Practices in Clayoquot Sound. This panel agreed that in principle the "world is interconnected at all levels; attempts to understand it entail analyzing its components and considering the whole system" (Bunnell and Atleo 1995, 25).

The Scientific Panel's adoption of the principle of interconnectedness represents a paradigmatic shift that has implications for the assumptions of scientific methodology. The idea that meaningful relationships between variables are determined by mathematical significance has been called into question. Ordinarily, in the physical sciences, when mathematical significance cannot be found between variables, scientists conclude that such variables are not related even if the variables are juxtaposed in time or space. As my logical-positivist professor said to me rhetorically: "Just because two birds fly together, does that mean that they are related?" However, according to the assumptions of the theory of Tsawalk, "significance" can imply meanings beyond the measure of current mathematical models. The critical assumption of Tsawalk is that there is a unity, or meaningful interrelationship, between all the variables of existence, whereas the dominant scientific methodology assumes that variables are not significantly related unless proven otherwise.

For example, traditional Nuu-chah-nulth people have understood for millennia (without the benefit of modern meteorological science) that during a certain season, morning dew in and around the village site is directly related to specific weather patterns miles offshore in the Pacific Ocean. Urbanized young people who may not believe that two birds flying together are related and who do not listen to their elders have been known to go out fishing and run into a storm predicted by the morning dew. A number of reliable signs have proven to be accurate predictors of forthcoming weather conditions, such as a doughnut-shaped ring of white cloud around the middle of a local cone-shaped mountain. When this cloud formation appears in a specific season and during a particular time of day, a gale-force weather pattern can be expected offshore the following day.

The relationship between morning dew and offshore weather patterns falls into the empirical, observational realm of human experience. Over time it has proven to be as reliable as scientific data even though it may not be amenable to current scientific instruments of measurement. As humans alter the climatic conditions of earth, these data may also be altered, and new weather patterns may emerge that can also be read as reliably as the old patterns. The major difficulty with, and limitation of, contemporary research is that current methodologies do not, or perhaps as yet cannot, cope with the multiple variables presented by a theoretical assumption of the unity of all things. Today the strongest and most reliable research data come from experiments that are limited to an examination of two or three variables. In contrast, those on the Scientific Panel went much farther in stating that the "world is interconnected at all levels." It appears that two birds flying together might be related after all. These empirically related observations about the nature of creation have also been made in the field that is now known as social science.

Applications to Social Science
At first glance Tsawalk and other social science theories may not seem to differ because both kinds of theories may often rely upon a context of conditions for analytical purposes. As noted earlier, Tsawalk was originally conceived as a theory of context since each variable under investigation was hypothesized to be affected by a variety of social, political, economic, and historical conditions. In this respect the theory does not appear to offer anything new to the field. However, what is new about it is its theoretical assumption based upon an underlying worldview that is all-inclusive of existence and human experiences. In this theory, what science may have once considered immaterial, such as the spiritual realm, is more "real" than what science considers material, the physical realm. If this theoretical assumption about the nature of reality – that the immaterial is more substantive than the material – is subjected to experimentation and subsequently found to have some credence, then this could have serious implications for social, public, and other relevant human policies because the reality of the spiritual dimension also includes a moral, or value, dimension. It is the *value* dimension of existence that poses the most serious implications for Western culture. For example, the human value of *generosity,* according to Nuu-chah-nulth lived experience, can be considered part of the original design of creation and is therefore as much of a natural law as any known physical law. Moreover, when Qua-ootz is considered as the Creator, *isaak* (respect for all life forms) also becomes a natural and original design of creation.

In contrast, the predominant scientific worldview based in Darwinian theory postulates that biodiversity evolved through a random process of evolution. In this view life forms developed through a process of survival-of-the-fittest or through a process known as natural selection. This means that some life forms cannot be fit to survive and so are selected out while others are selected in. It follows logically then that dominance, strength, superiority, and survival are the natural and original designs of creation.

Included in the Nuu-chah-nulth worldview, it must be remembered, is a belief in the existence of Qua-ootz, Owner of Creation. The meta-context for all research driven by the theory of Tsawalk is the presence and role of Qua-ootz. For millennia the principles presented in origin stories were verified through the practice of *oosumich* and applied in daily life and ceremonial potlatches, resulting in societies that managed, for the most part, to balance the rights of individuals and groups as well as the rights of humans and the other life forms. Yes, there were occasional failures, some warfare, and evil policies and practices, but there were also policies and practices that had outcomes conducive to the well-being of competing life forms. In general, it is my indigenous perspective that the Americas were pristine prior to contact less due to nature, as might be assumed by newcomers, and more due to sound and deliberate management. The Nuu-chah-nulth orchestrated this management by means of chiefly sovereign rights to *hahuulthi* (ancestral territory), which were recognized by all neighbouring nations. For the most part, these are neither completely indigenous observations nor indigenous romanticizations, as some will claim, but early observations made by various explorers and missionaries during the 1600s.

I have tested the theory of Tsawalk twice in the field of educational research. In the mid-1980s I completed a doctoral dissertation entitled "Grade 12 Enrolments of Status Indians in British Columbia: 1949-1985." And in 1993 I completed another study, "An Examination of Native Education in British Columbia: Kindergarten Readiness and Self-Image and Academic Achievement of Grades 4 to 12." Both studies assume that numerous social, political, and economic variables meaningfully affect educational performance. When these variables are prevailingly negative or oppressive, educational performance will also be prevailingly negative. Both studies lend some credence to the theory.

For example, it might reasonably be thought that elementary school students go about their lives relatively unaffected by broad social issues. They appear to be more interested in their own trends and immediate concerns. However, Harry Wolcott, in a study of a small, rural First Nations school in British Columbia during the late 1950s and early 1960s, found that his elementary school students admitted to aspiring to become doctors, lawyers, and teachers but were certain that their only future would be patterned after the dismal lives of their parents. In another study, conducted by Harry Hawthorn in 1966 and 1967, the failure rate of First Nations students in grades 1 to 12 nationwide was an astronomical 94 percent. This study replicated Wolcott's finding in that First Nations students appeared not to aspire to any future beyond the experience of their parents. First Nations students did appear to respond negatively to oppressive social, political, and economic environments.

Would students respond differently to more positive social, political, and economic environments? In my 1993 study, elementary school students in both rural and urban areas, almost without exception and *without qualification*, aspired to every sort of job and profession. One fourth-grade girl could not decide whether she wanted to be a Supreme Court judge or the prime minister of Canada.

These changes in student performance and aspirations are predicted by the theory of Tsawalk in the following way: When socio-political conditions are prevailingly negative, it is expected that educational performance and aspirations will also be negative, and when socio-political conditions are prevailingly positive, educational performance and aspirations will also be positive. Indices of negative socio-political conditions for First Nations people were widespread during the 1950s and 1960s, and these conditions coincided with negative educational performance and negative aspirations. Since 1972, when the federal government accepted the National Indian Brotherhood's education proposal, entitled "Indian Control of Indian Education," the socio-political climate for First Nations people in Canada has improved considerably, augmented in 1982 by the constitutional entrenchment of Aboriginal Rights and in 1997 by the decision in *Delgamuukw v. British Columbia* to recognize oral histories as legally admissible evidence. These measures have facilitated an increase in educational performance among First Nations students and contributed to a positive set of job and professional aspirations. At the time of the research, completed in the late 1980s, the conclusions were necessarily tentative because of the continuing dominance of the more classical scientific theories, such as logical positivism, which insist that variables be proven to be significantly and empirically related before any validity can be claimed. However, at the dawn of the twenty-first century, the types of conclusions indicated by the research have become more commonplace.

For example, over millennia the Nuu-chah-nulth have made reliable observations within the affective-value domain of human experience. Generosity is an affective value. The theory of Tsawalk predicts that it may be possible to articulate generosity in the same way that gravity as a natural law is articulated. This assumption about the nature of creation, if confirmed by research, has grave and radical implications. State, provincial, and federal laws affecting building codes, speed limits on highways, aircraft airlanes in the skies, take-off and approach air speeds, and so on are in the main dependent upon the law of gravity and other known natural laws. What is the point? If affective values can be experimentally shown to be natural laws, these too must surely and eventually have an impact on social, political, and economic policies and practices. At this point in human history, affective values are recognized as valid not in the mainstream of life, which is dominated by the acquisition of wealth, but on the margins of Western society. Affective values do not inform the central areas of postsecondary study but are left, for the most part, to the marginalized religious institutions.

For example, the law of generosity may be stated as follows: It is necessary to give in order to receive. According to this law it is not better to give than to receive because both giving and receiving are equivalent and interactive values. Consequently generosity can be viewed as a natural law of reciprocity. The ancient Nuu-chah-nulth felt so strongly about the importance of the relationship between generosity and the quality of life that the opposite of generosity was equated with death. For example, a lazy person is not generous and thus does not contribute to family and community wellbeing. Lazy people cannot participate in the law of reciprocity because they produce nothing. People who constantly refused to contribute were eventually left to fend for themselves. Shunning, abandonment, and expulsion from community were all equivalent to death, or at least to a meaningless life, while maintaining relationships through acts of generosity were equated with a meaningful life.

The collective Nuu-chah-nulth experience teaches not only that a generous person is never without the necessities of life, but also that the act of giving generates a sense of personal wellbeing, a sense of balance and harmony. Generosity, when enacted, seems to have its own consequences in the same way that the activation of natural laws has natural consequences. Allow a china cup to slip from your hands, and the law of gravity ensures that it shatters on the marble floor. The difference between the china-cup experience and the act-of-generosity experience is timing. In the former the outcome is immediate, while in the latter the act of reciprocity may be delayed and not necessarily or apparently empirically connected to the initial act of generosity. Nevertheless, for those accustomed to the ways and consequences of generosity, such an act can have immediate personal returns. The act of giving can feel good. It can provide a sense of wellbeing. It may tend to strengthen human ties. All these statements can be translated into propositions and tested.

For example, a survey may find a significant difference between the experiences of those who are habitual givers, those who are occasional givers, and those who never give unless pressured. Longitudinal studies will deny or support the proposition that habitual givers are never without the essentials. Since the time of contact the Western way of life has unwaveringly produced a class of people so poor that they become homeless beggars subject to death by starvation, privation, exposure, neglect, or any number of otherwise curable diseases. If research shows that affective values are natural laws, the death of poor people in wealthy cities becomes a violation of these natural laws.

Perhaps, in the context of today's highly conflicted world, no social science studies can be more important than those that test *isaak* (respect for all life forms). *Isaak* is predicated upon the notion that every life form has intrinsic value and that this should be recognized through appropriate protocols of interaction. Consequently, nations recognize other nations and forge treaties with each other. The Nuu-chah-nulth recognize and respect the salmon with ceremony. The wolf recognizes the deer and demonstrates respect by not violating the deer's innards. Traditional Nuu-chah-nulth hunters follow the same protocol with the deer. *Isaak*, as another law of life, promotes balance and harmony within creation. It is possible to develop a series of propositions that can be tested using social science methodologies. First, what does *isaak* mean in practice? It means that life forms of every kind are held in equal esteem. All life forms have intrinsic value. Humans of every race have equal value, as do the deer, the wolf, the whale, the eagle, the cedar tree. Holding life forms in equal esteem demands that balance and harmony be maintained among them by the development of protocols. Research methods can be developed to test the proposition that respectful protocols between life forms tend to promote balance and harmony.

Although the philosophical foundation of the theory of Tsawalk differs from the evolution-based philosophical foundations of Western science, the theory of Tsawalk, at this point in time, must utilize the same research methods, strategies, and measurement instruments as other theories. The major difference is found in the interpretation of what constitutes significance. Whereas other theories may assume that if variables do not show significant relationships, these variables are not related or connected to each other, the theory of Tsawalk always assumes a meaningful relationship between variables.

Although the theory of Tsawalk may never be completely substantiated because of human limitations, it does provide opportunities for research from an indigenous perspective. We claim to be holistic thinkers, and we now have the theoretical means to put such thinking into practice. Tsawalk is not a new perspective but as old as time itself. It is based upon origin stories about cultural heroes like Raven and Aint-tin-mit. It is a theory not only about how light did not originate in the physical world, but also about the origin of light. Tsawalk is based upon perspectives about the beginnings of all things. In this respect, it is a theory of beginnings and possibly a theory of everything. In the meantime, relatively small theories can be developed from the theory of Tsawalk, theories about small connections and relationships not previously considered. If everything truly is one (*heshook-ish tsawalk*), then more and more of this unity has yet to be discovered.

Epilogue

The first peoples' struggles to orient themselves according to creation's original design, as recounted in origin stories, parallel the current struggles of indigenous peoples to orient themselves according to the contradictions of the postmodern world, which espouses pluralism but cannot find balance and harmony between multiple, competing interests. The theory of Tsawalk offers an alternative stance from which to view contemporary problem solving because it assumes the unity of creation irrespective of any of contemporary society's contradictions. Creation and destruction, good and evil, competing individual and group interests are all part of an original design. The ancient Nuu-chah-nulth came to understand some of the mystery of *heshook-ish tsawalk*. They came to understand the value of the individual without necessarily undermining the value of the group. They understood the value in life and the value in death, the value in love and the value in pain. Can such understanding be achieved again?

When Aint-tin-mit came back to earth to create biodiversity, there was natural resistance to the threat of change. Just as the means of resistance employed then (the weapons made by Raccoon and Deer) were used to facilitate change, so too will the contemporary tools of resistance (language and scholarship) become the very means of change and transformation within indigenous societies. The authority of such scholarship will not, and cannot, rest with any contemporary intellectual giant (a figure common to Western scholarship). Rather, the authority will rest with the tried perspectives and practices of ancient heritages. The content of this scholarship will be based upon some of the best origin stories, such as the ones about Raven and Aint-tin-mit, the analysis of which may eventually serve to guide not only their First Nations owners but also the *mamulthni* (those who, according to the

Nuu-chah-nulth, were originally regarded as visitors without land because they came in ships outfitted like houseboats) toward a more balanced and harmonious way of life. These visitors have made their gifts
of science and technology evident and recognizable to all, while our
gifts of relationality and *isaak* (respect for all life forms) have only now
begun to emerge. Hopefully, in an increasingly fragmented world, these
gifts can help us all to *tloo-qua-nah.*

Notes

Introduction

1 According to traditional Nuu-chah-nulth beliefs, experiences, and practices, reality is the sum total of existence and includes both the physical universe and the spiritual realm.

2 A reference to cultural ways of life that have substantive roots in the precontact indigenous past.

Chapter 1: *Tsawalk*

1 "Chief" is a Western term that equates to a political leader today. The original meaning was inclusive of leadership in all dimensions of human reality: the social, political, economic, and spiritual.

Chapter 2: *Utla*

1 The Nuu-chah-nulth placename "Ahous" refers to the original village site of the Ahousaht people on Vargas Island, currently uninhabited. "Ahousaht" is located on Flores Island, on the Maaqtusiis land reserve. The word "Ahousaht" actually means "people of Ahous" (similarly, Hesquiaht and Cla-o-qui-aht translate as "people of Hesqui" and "people of Cla-o-qui" respectively) but this misunderstanding of the name by English-speaking government officials was carried into government documents and consequently Ahousaht is now a placename.

Chapter 5: *Suh-tcha*

1 The life and order of the spiritual realm is a profound subject that was well known to the ancient Nuu-chah-nulth, but this information is likely not as well known to many modern Nuu-chah-nulth.

2 Ahousaht historian John Jacobson's personal letter to Wilson Duff (on file with the author).

3 *Robinson Crusoe*, by Daniel Defoe, was and is a text that has been studied in elementary schools everywhere. It is one example of the Hobbesian view of early Aboriginal life.

4 Maaqtusiis is the contemporary spelling of Marktosis.

Chapter 6: *Nuu-pooh*

1 Full-scale war is not to be confused with personal feuds, boundary-dispute skir-
mishes, or youthful and temporary forays into forbidden territories, none of
which are classified as wars by historians. The Ahousaht-Otoosaht War was a
full-scale war of annihilation that took place during the early part of the 1800s.

Bibliography

Arima, Eugene Y. 1983. *The West Coast People: The Nootka of Vancouver Island and Cape Flattery.* Victoria, BC: British Columbia Provincial Museum.

Atleo, E. Richard. 1990. "Grade 12 Enrolments of Status Indians in British Columbia: 1949-1985." EdD dissertation. Department of Administrative, Adult and Higher Education, University of British Columbia, Vancouver.

–. 1993. "An Examination of Native Education in British Columbia: Kindergarten Readiness and Self-Image and Academic Achievement of Grades 4 to 12." Vancouver: Native Brotherhood of British Columbia.

Barrow, John D. 1990. *Theories of Everything: The Quest for Ultimate Explanation.* London: Vintage. Reprint 1991.

Berry, Thomas. 1988. *The Dream of the Earth.* San Francisco: Sierra Club Books.

Blumberg, Baruch. 2000. "Nature's R_x." Interview with Joel L. Swerdlow. *National Geographic* 197, 4 (April): 98-117.

Brown, Joseph Epes. 1986. *The Spiritual Legacy of the American Indian.* New York: Crossroads.

Brumbaugh, Robert S., and Nathaniel M. Lawrence. 1963. *Philosophers on Education: Six Essays on the Foundations of Western Thought.* Boston: Houghton Mifflin Company.

Bunnell, Fred, and E. Richard Atleo. 1995. *The Scientific Panel for Sustainable Forest Practices in Clayoquot Sound: First Nations' Perspectives Relating to Forest Practices Standards in Clayoquot Sound.* Report. Victoria, BC: Cortex Consultants.

Capra, Fritjof. 1991. *The Tao of Physics: An Exploration of the Parallels between Modern Physics and Eastern Mysticism.* 3rd ed. Glasgow: Caledonian International Book Manufacturing.

Clutesi, George. 1969. *Potlatch.* Sidney, BC: Gray's Publishing.

Defoe, Daniel. 1991. *Robinson Crusoe.* Toronto: Bantam Books.

Delgamuukw v. British Columbia. File No. 23799, 16-17 June and 11 December 1997.

Duff, Wilson. 1965. *The Indian History of British Columbia.* Vol. 1, *The Impact of the White Man.* Victoria, BC: Royal British Columbia Museum.

Erdoes, Richard, and Alfonso Ortiz, eds. 1999. *American Indian Trickster Tales.* New York: Penguin Books.

Eysenck, M.W. 1984. *A Handbook of Cognitive Psychology.* London: Erlbaum.

Fisher, Robin. 1977. *Contact and Conflict: Indian-European Relations in British Columbia, 1774-1890*. Vancouver: UBC Press.

Gisday Wa and Delgam Uukw. 1992. *The Spirit in the Land: Statements of the Gitksan and Wet'suwet'en Hereditary Chiefs in the Supreme Court of British Columbia, 1987-1990*. Gabriola, BC: Reflections.

Hawthorn, H.B., ed. 1966. *A Survey of the Contemporary Indians of Canada*. Vol. 1. Ottawa: Indian Affairs Branch.

–, ed. 1967. *A Survey of the Contemporary Indians of Canada*. Vol. 2. Ottawa: Indian Affairs Branch.

Hobbes, Thomas. 1651. *Leviathan*, edited by A.P. Martinich. Peterborough, ON: Broadview Press.

Hodgson, Janet, and Jay Kothare. 1990. *Vision Quest: Native Spirituality and the Church in Canada*. Toronto: Anglican Book Centre.

Jaenen, C.J. 1986. "Education for Francization: The Case of New France in the Seventeenth Century." In *Indian Education in Canada*. Vol. 1, *The Legacy*, edited by J. Barman, Y.M. Hebert, and D. McCaskill, 45-63. Vancouver: UBC Press.

Kane, Sean. 1998. *Wisdom of the Mythtellers*. Peterborough, ON: Broadview Press.

Kerlinger, F.N. 1973. *Foundations of Behavioural Research: Educational and Psychological Inquiry*. 2nd ed. New York: Holt, Rinehart and Winston.

Knight, Rolf. 1978. *Indians At Work: An Informal History of Native Indian Labour in British Columbia: 1858-1930*. Vancouver: New Star Books.

Knudtson, Peter, and David Suzuki. 1992. *Wisdom of the Elders*. Toronto: Stoddart.

Laslett, Peter, ed. 1993. *John Locke: Two Treatises of Government*. New York: Cambridge University Press.

Lewis, Thomas, Farci Amini, and Richard Lannon. *A General Theory of Love*. New York: Random House.

McEachern, Allan. 1991. *Delgamuukw et al. v. The Queen: Reasons for Judgment*. Smithers Registry No. 0843.

Moziño, José Mariano. 1970. *Noticias De Nutka: An Account of Nootka Sound 1792*. Translated and edited by Iris H. Wilson Engstrand. Vancouver: Douglas and McIntyre.

Neihardt, John G. 1972. *Black Elk Speaks: Being the Life Story of a Holy Man of the Oglala Sioux*. Lincoln, NB: University of Nebraska Press.

Ogbu, John U. 1987. "Variability in Minority School Performance: A Problem in Search of an Explanation." *Anthropology and Education Quarterly* 18, 4: 312-34.

Parkin, Alan J. 1987. *Memory and Amnesia: An Introduction*. Oxford: Basil Blackwell.

Penrose, Roger. 1993. *Shadows of the Mind*. London: Vintage.

Ritter, Alan, and Julia Conaway Bondanella, eds. 1988 [1651]. *Rousseau's Political Writings*. Translated by Julia Conaway Bondanella. New York: W.W. Norton and Co.

Saul, John Ralston. 1992. *Voltaire's Bastards: The Dictatorship of Reason in the West*. Toronto: Penguin Books.

Sproat, G.M. 1968. *The Nootka: Scenes and Studies of Savage Life*. Victoria, BC: Sono Nis Press. Reprint 1987.

Tarnas, Richard. 1991. *The Passion of the Western Mind: Understanding the Ideas That Have Shaped Our World View*. New York: Harmony Books.

Tully, James. 1994. *Strange Multiplicity: Constitutionalism in an Age of Diversity*. New York: Cambridge University Press.

Webb, Clement C.J. 1959. *A History of Philosophy.* Toronto: Oxford University Press.

Wolcott, Harry F. 1967. *A Kwakiutl Village and School.* San Francisco: Holt, Rinehart and Winston.

Zechmeister, E.B., and S.E. Nyberg. 1981. *Human Memory.* Monteray, CA: Brooks/Cole.

Index

Note: Page numbers in italics refer to illustrations.